Welcome to our happy and colorful word of coloring!
Unleash your creativity through relaxation while coloring these stunning mediation Dogs pattern. We created these 50 stunning classic dog-designs specifically for this book to help you find the balance of your life through creativity.

1. Break your pencils or colored pencils.
2. Turn off the phone, tablet, computer or any device.
3. Find your favorite page in the book and start coloring.
4. Try to focus on coloring, forget about your business. Use any color combinations or just your favorite colors. Enjoy the coloring process.
5. When you no longer want, stop.

Hope this lovely book help you find your self, relief your stress and make you happy.

Copyright © 2020 Yellow Cab Press

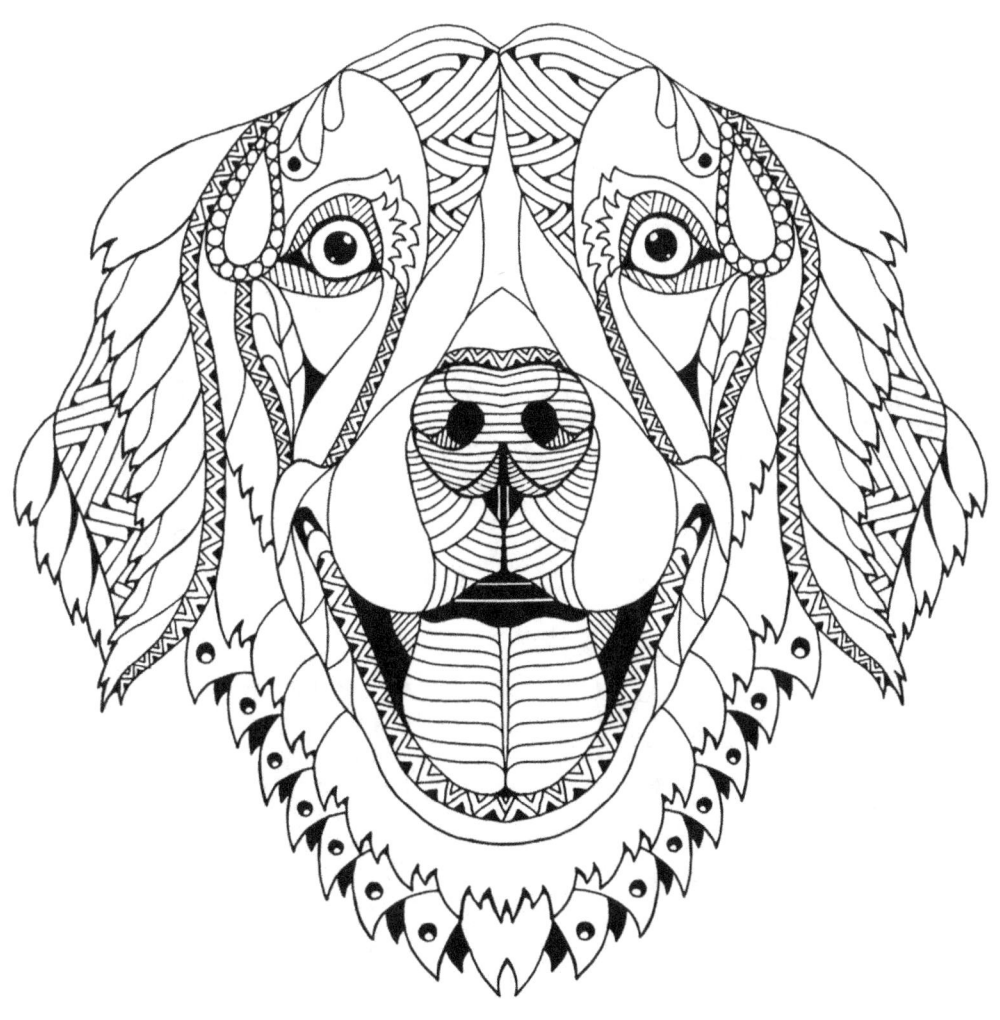

THIS BOOK BELONGS TO:

_____

Email:

_____

Phone Number:

_____

COLOR TEST PAGE

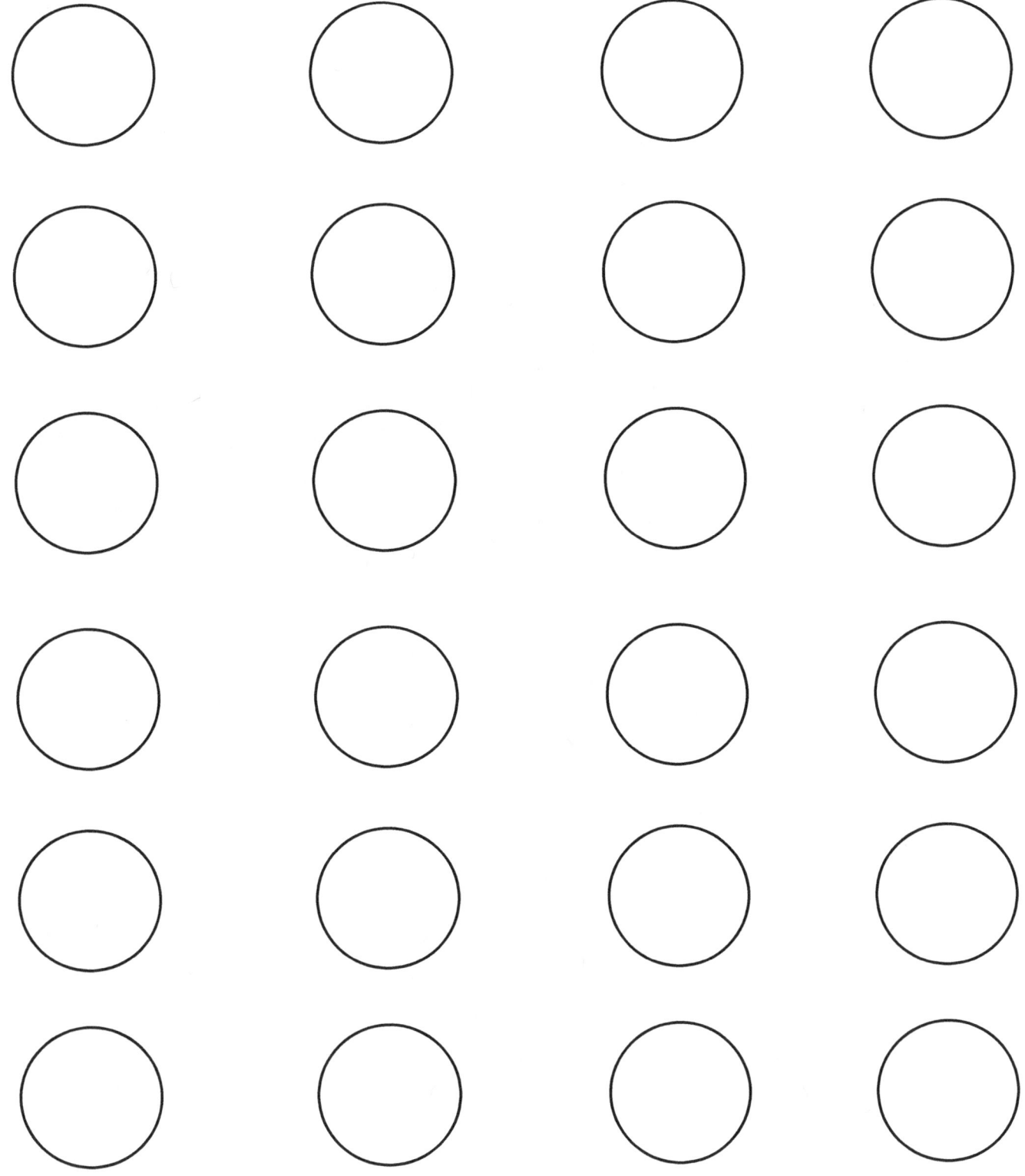

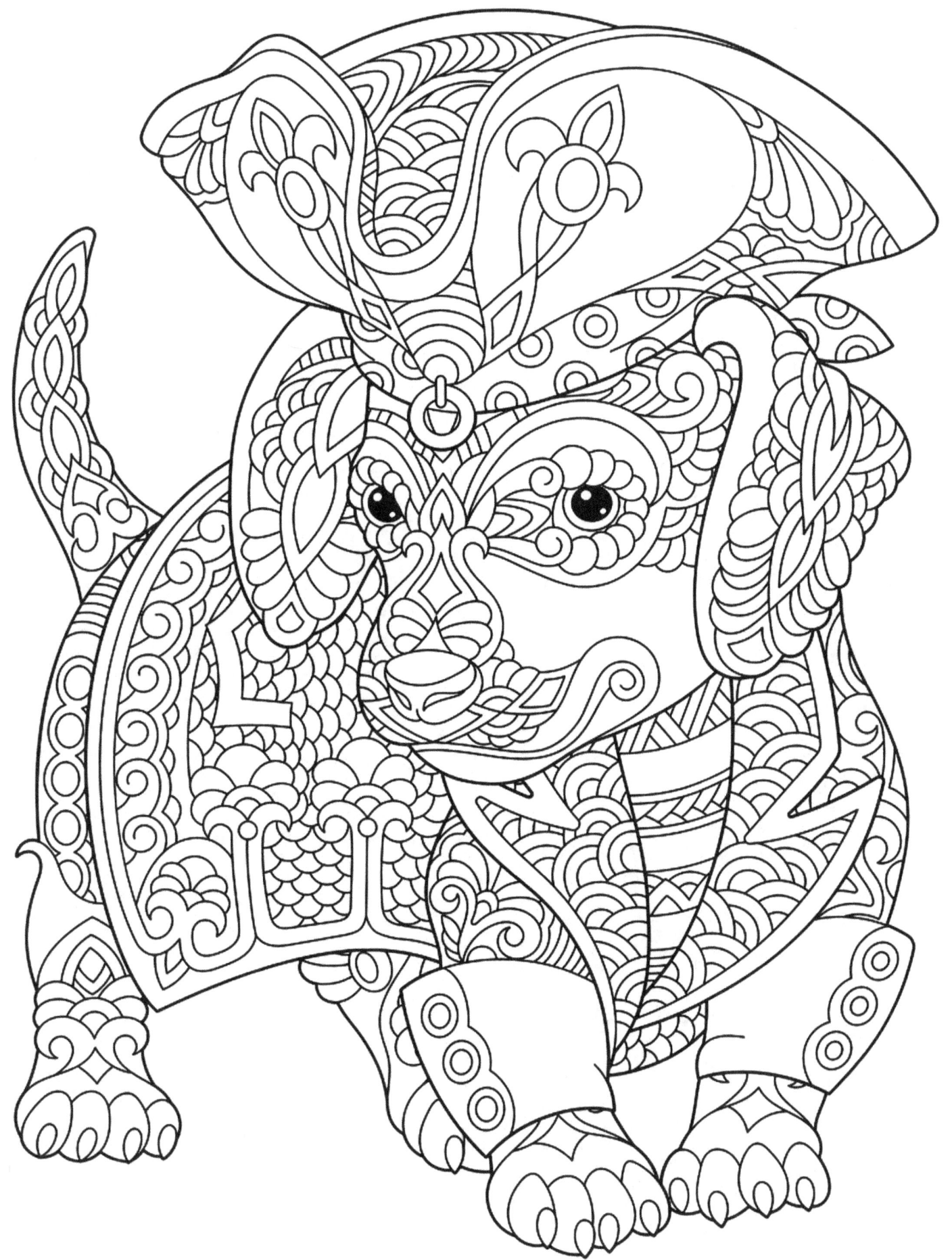

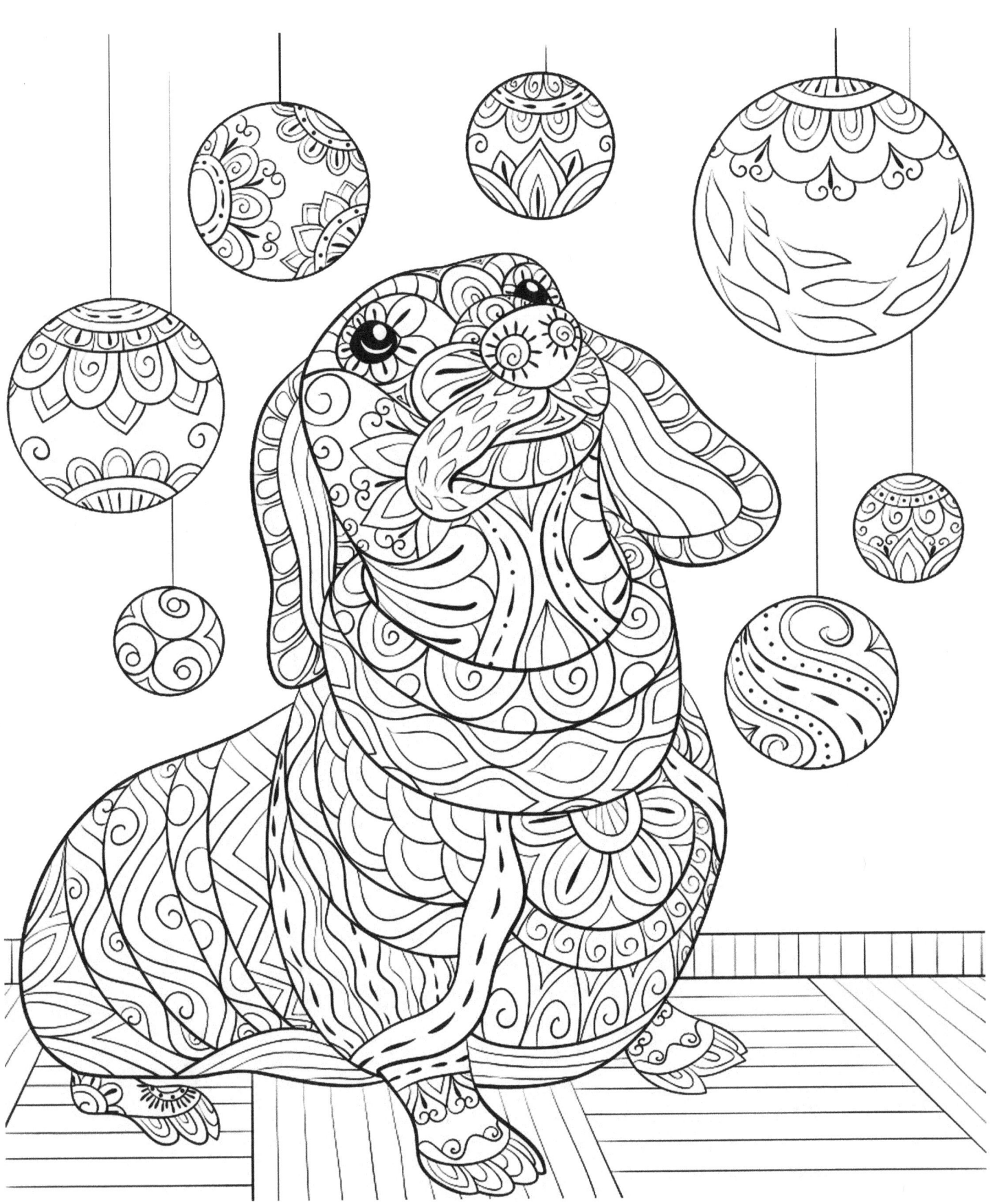

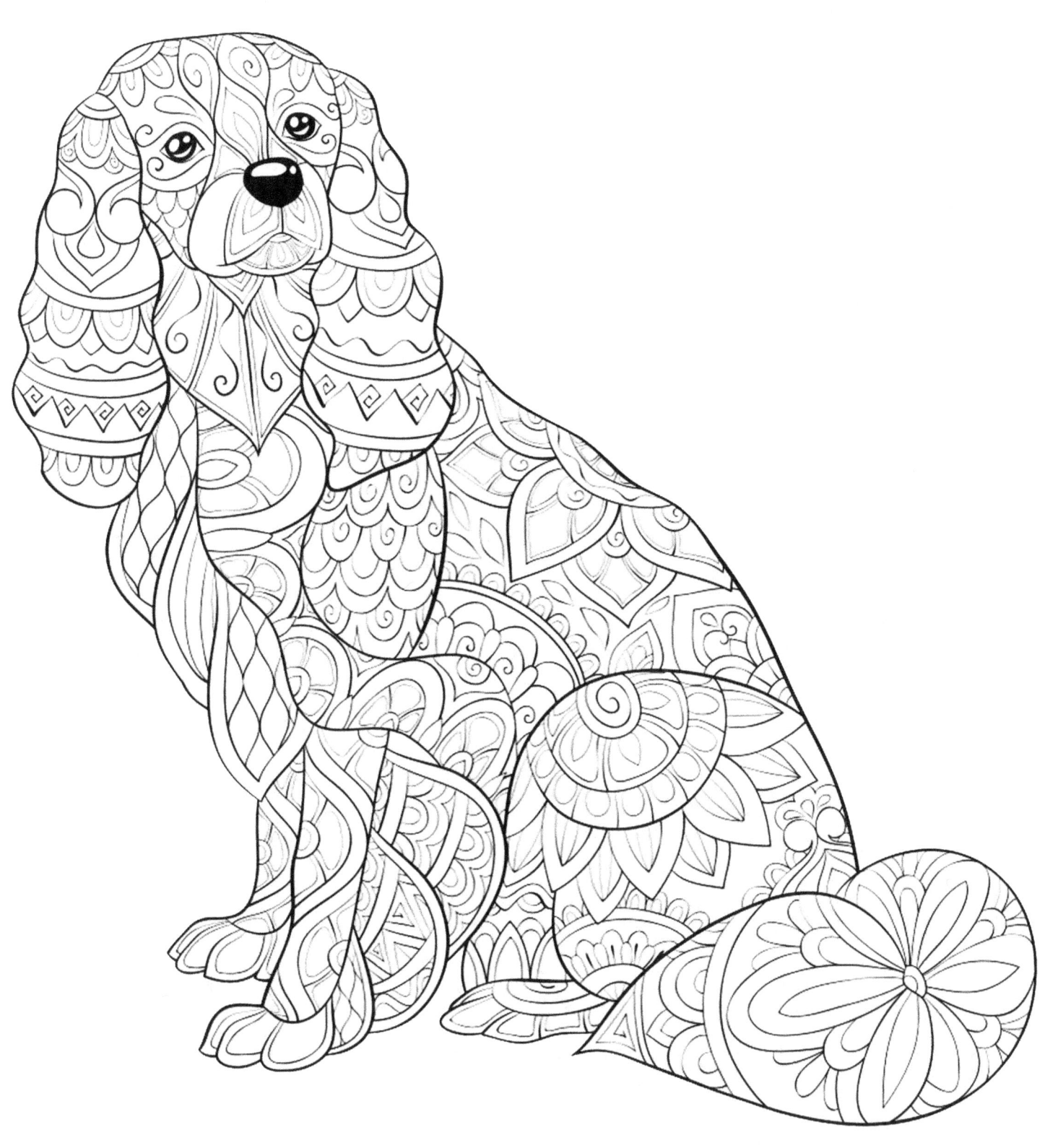

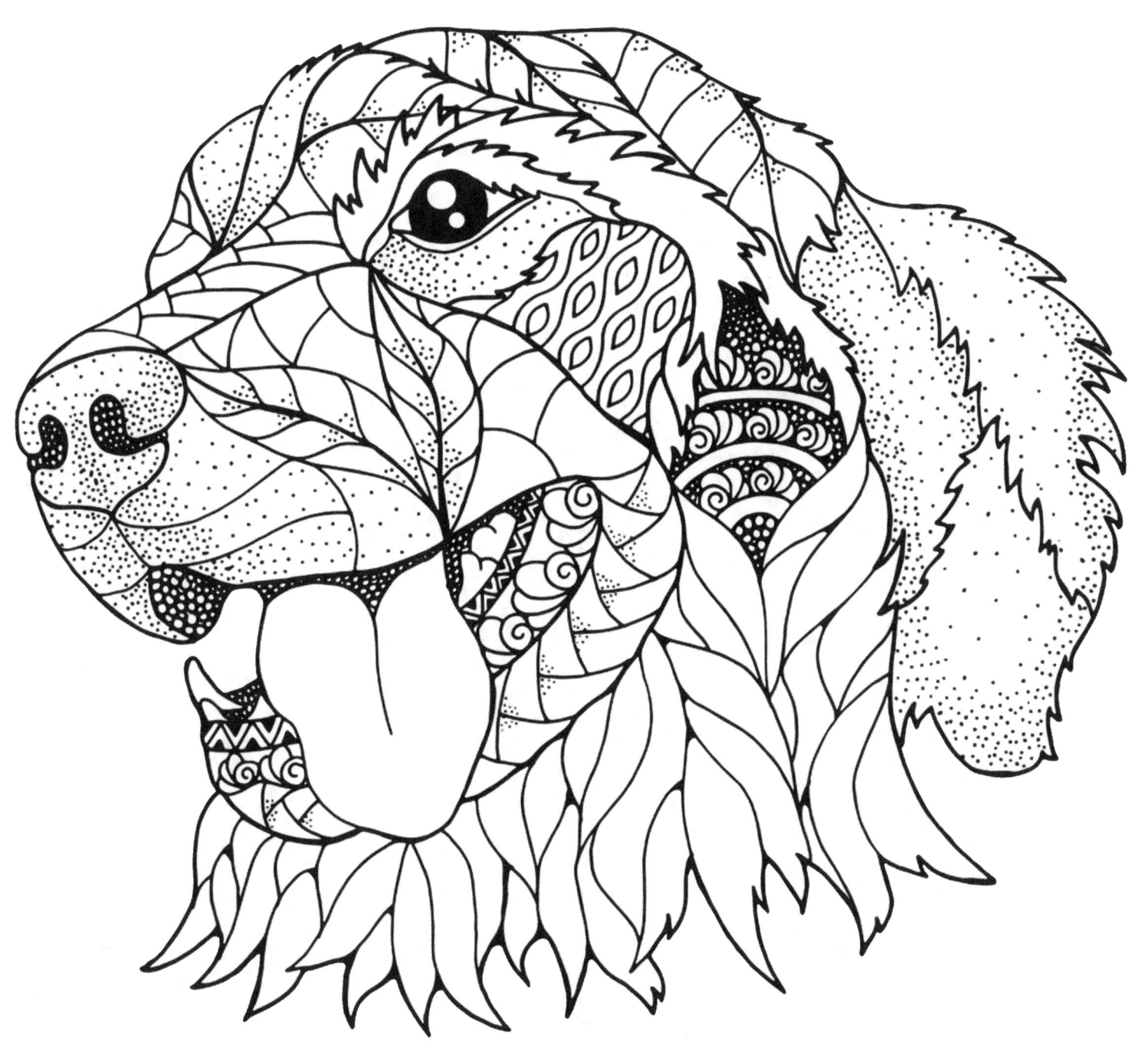

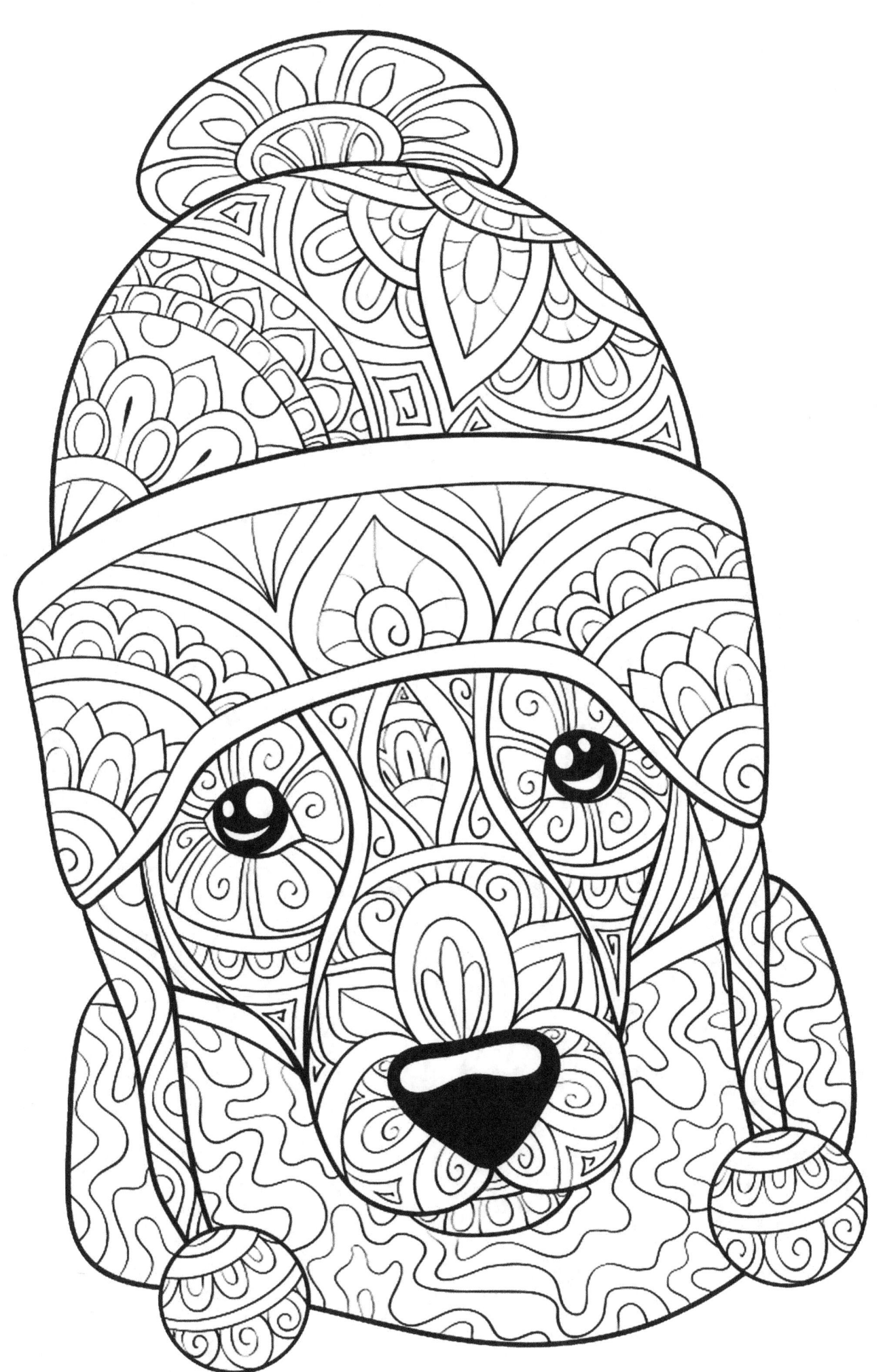

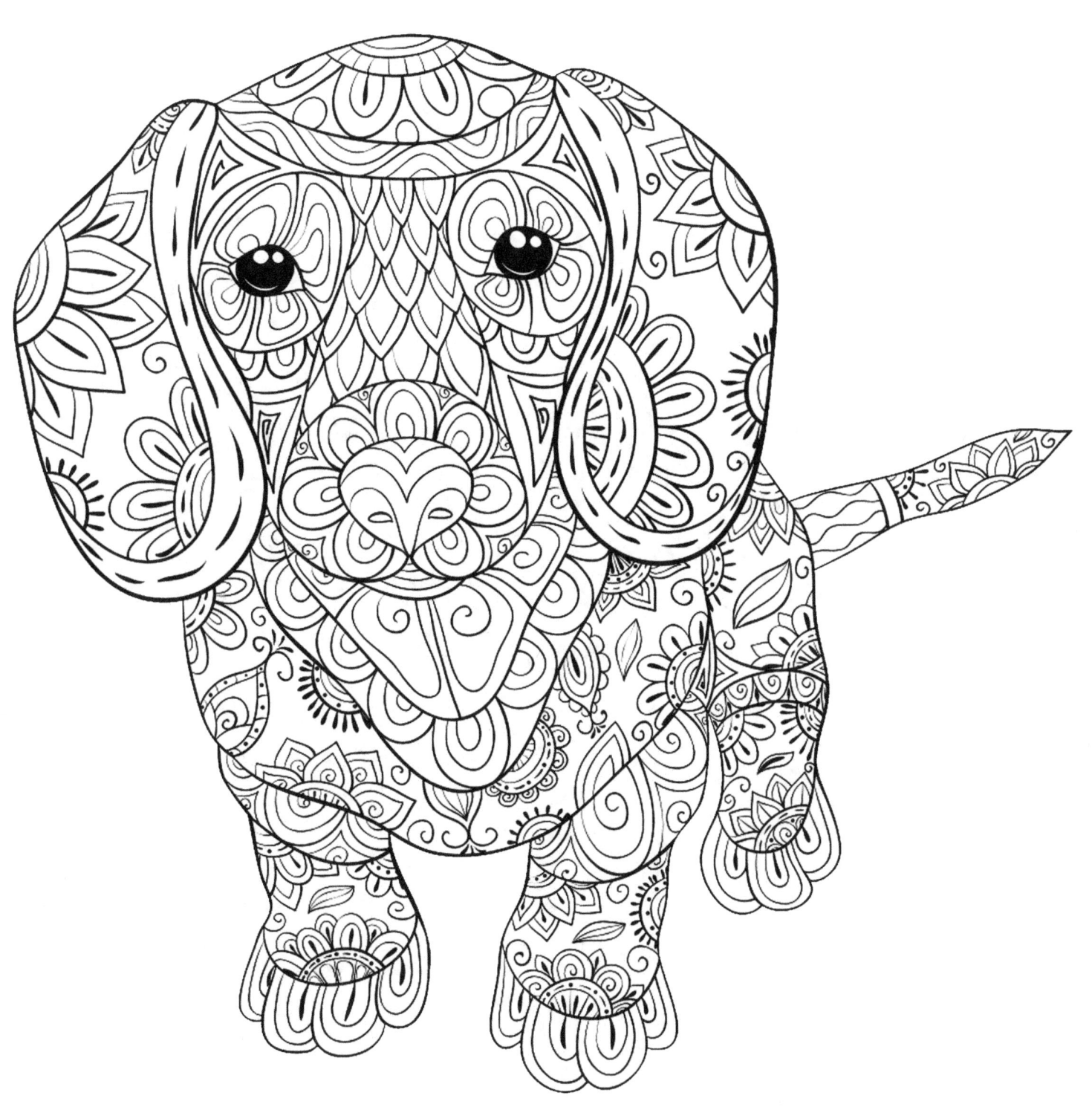

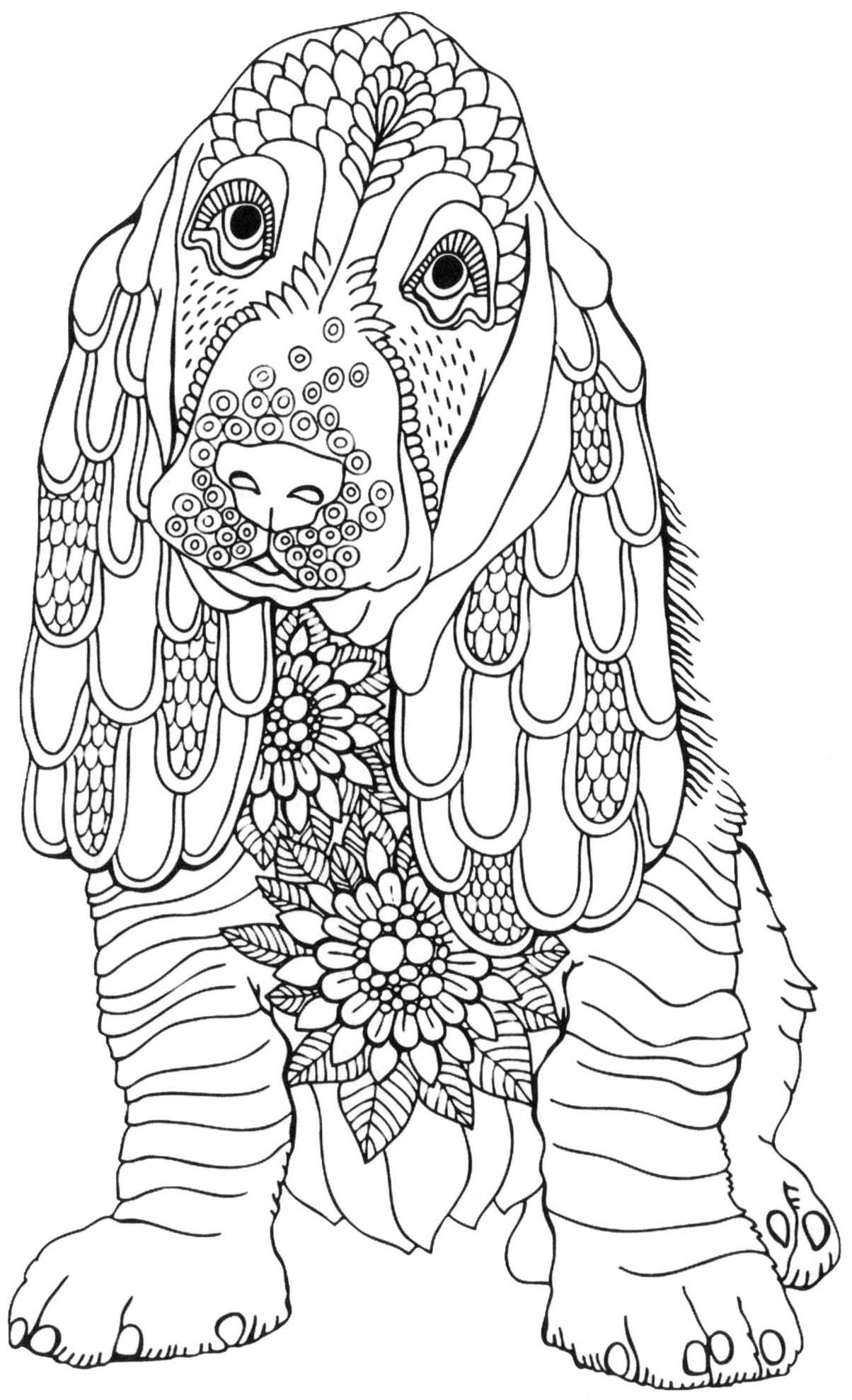

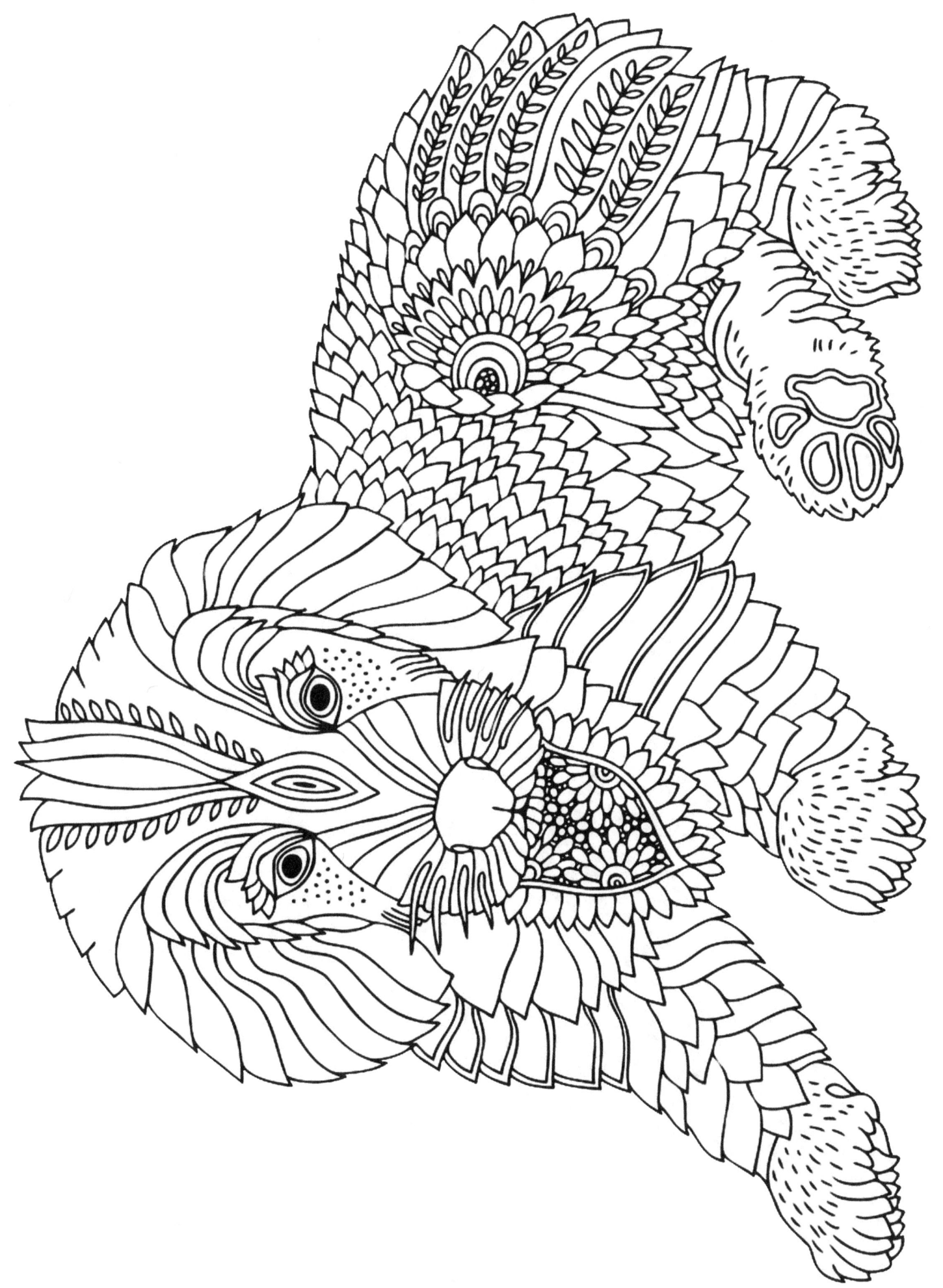

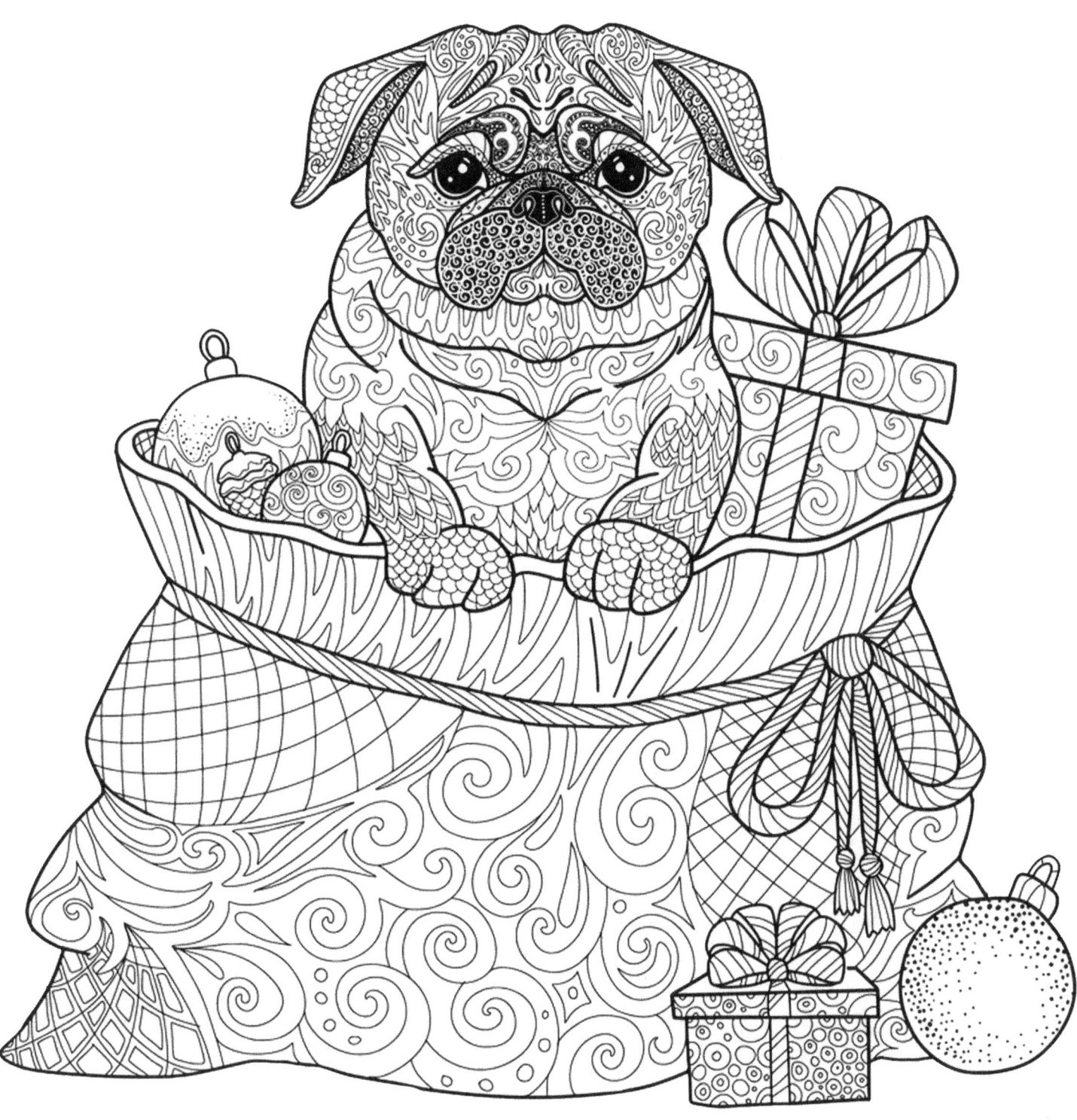

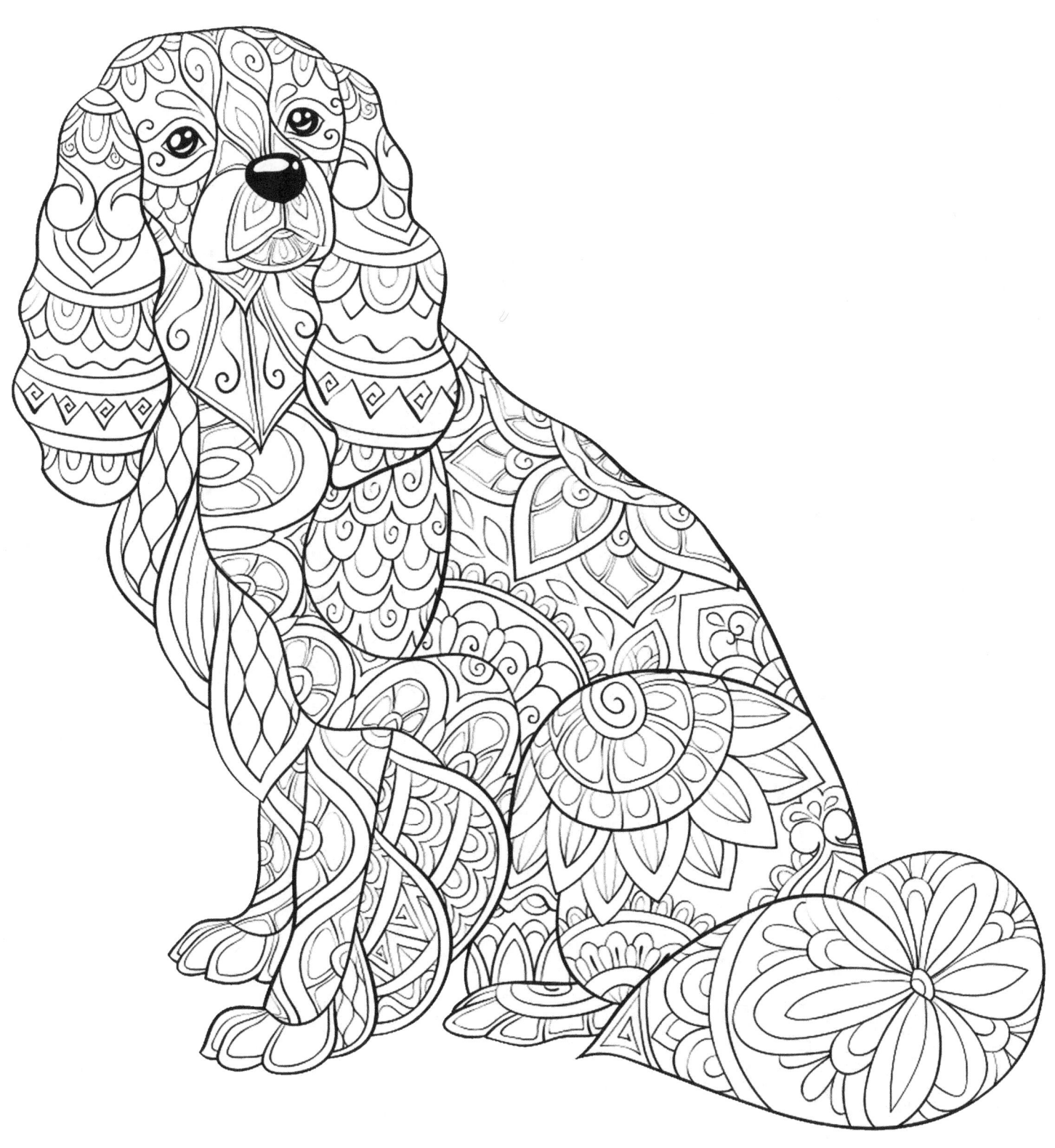

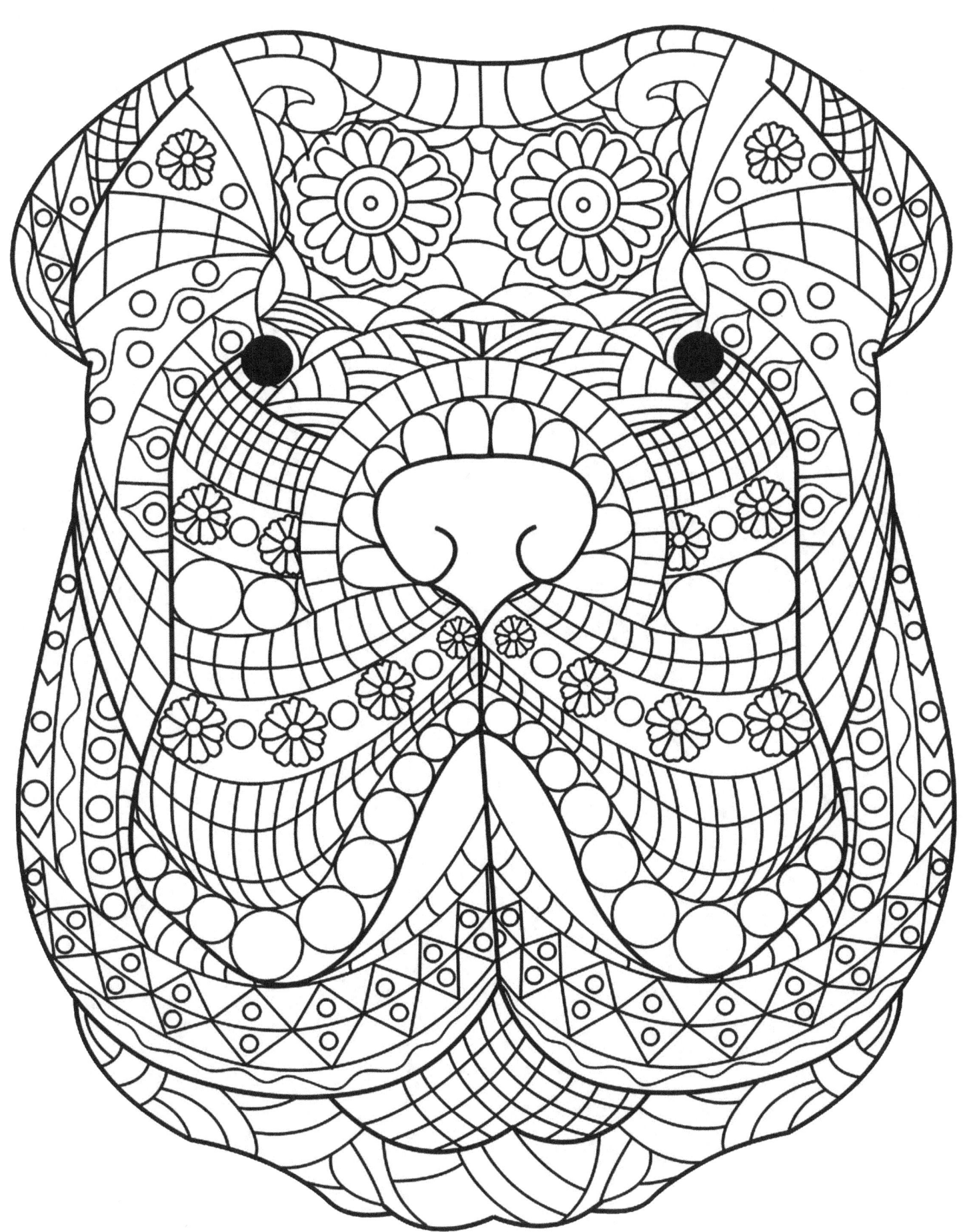

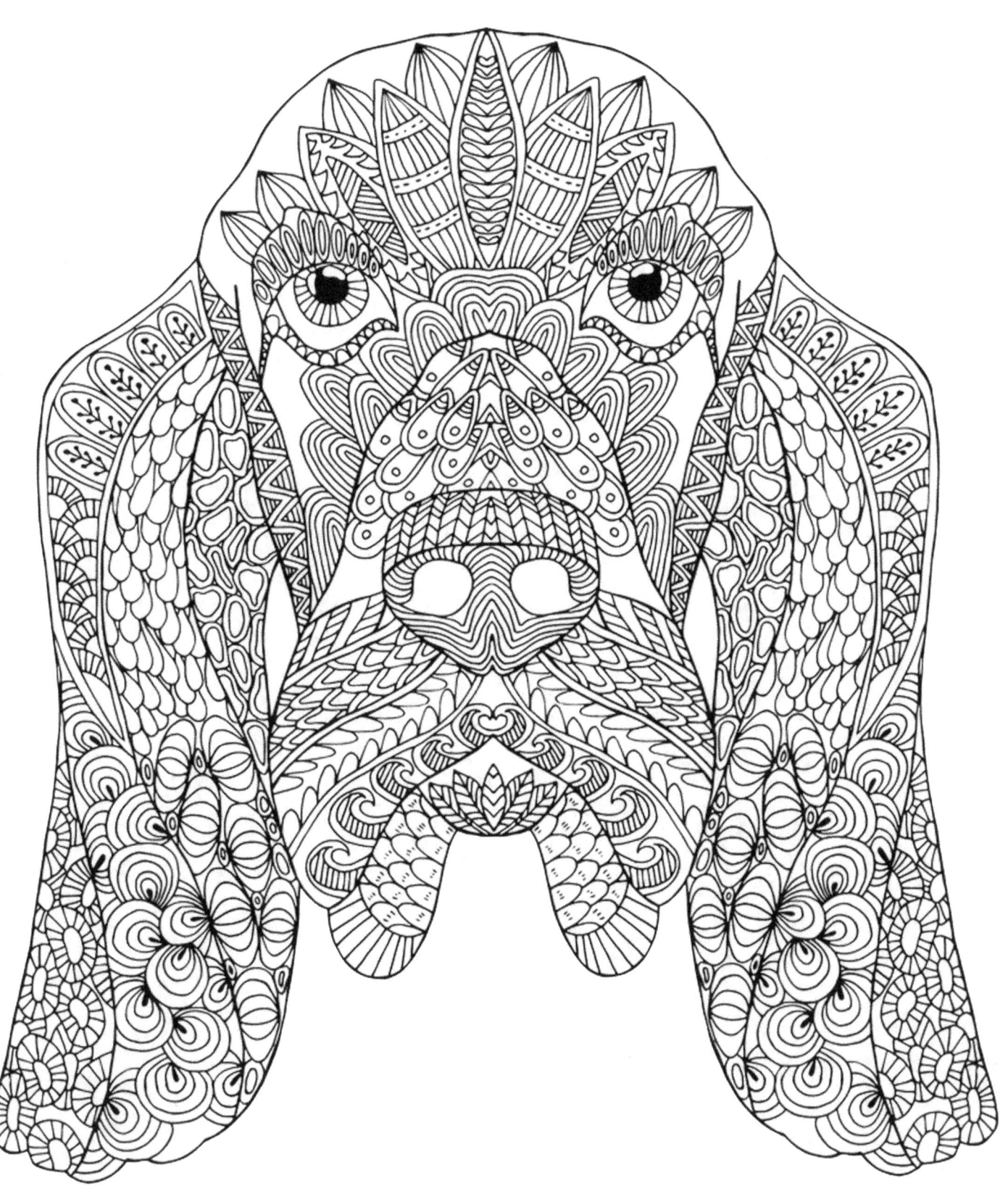

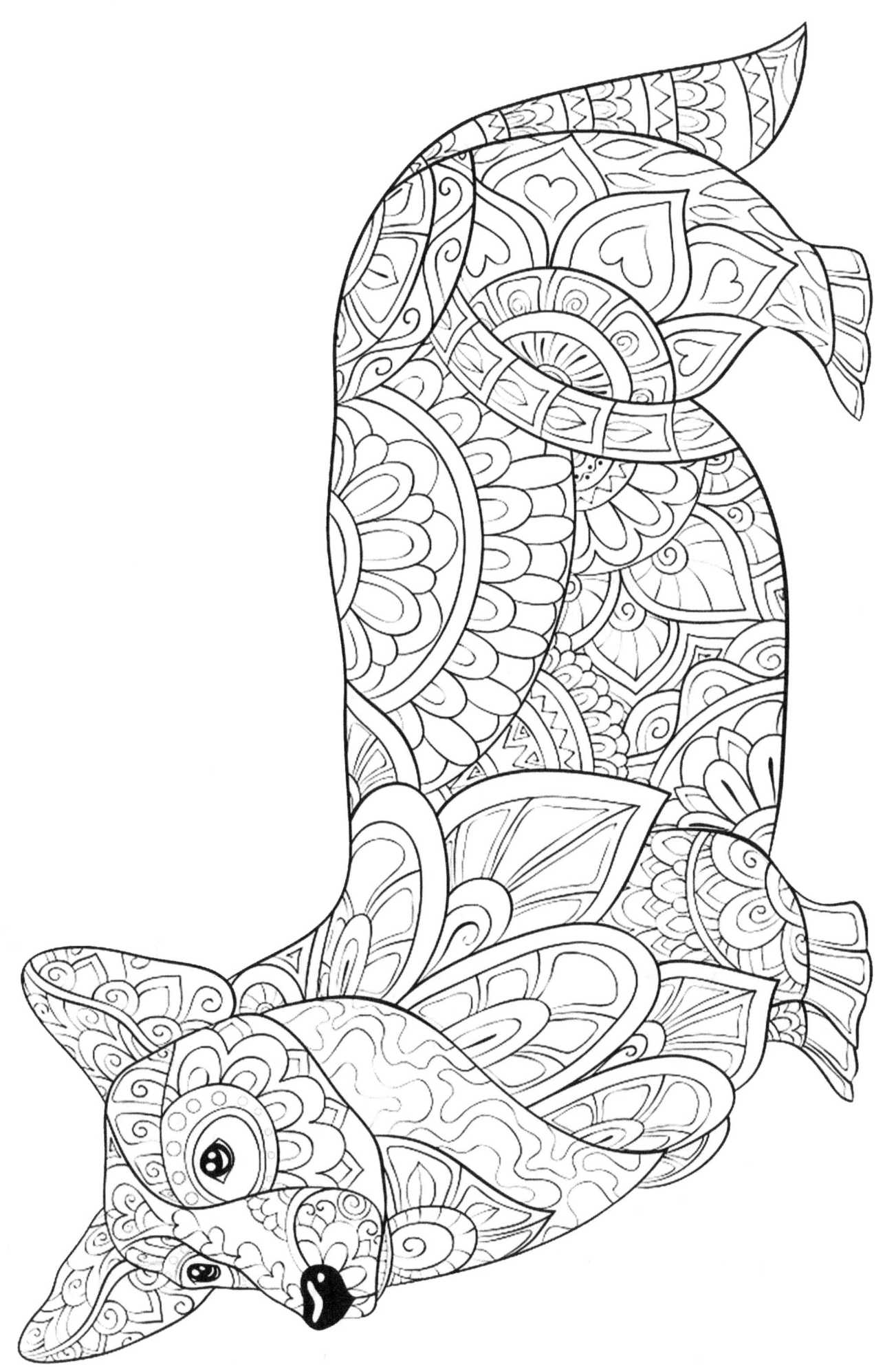

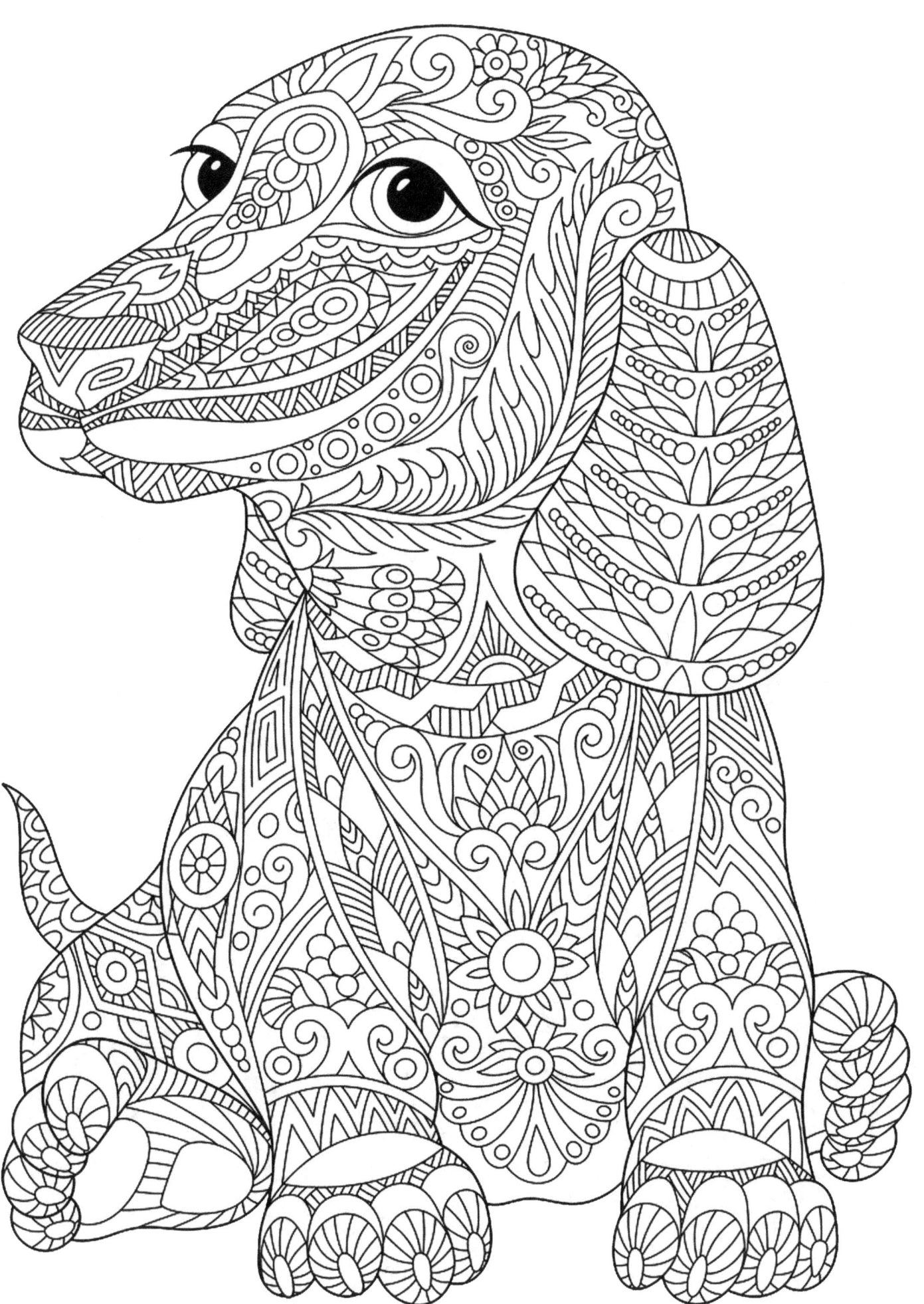

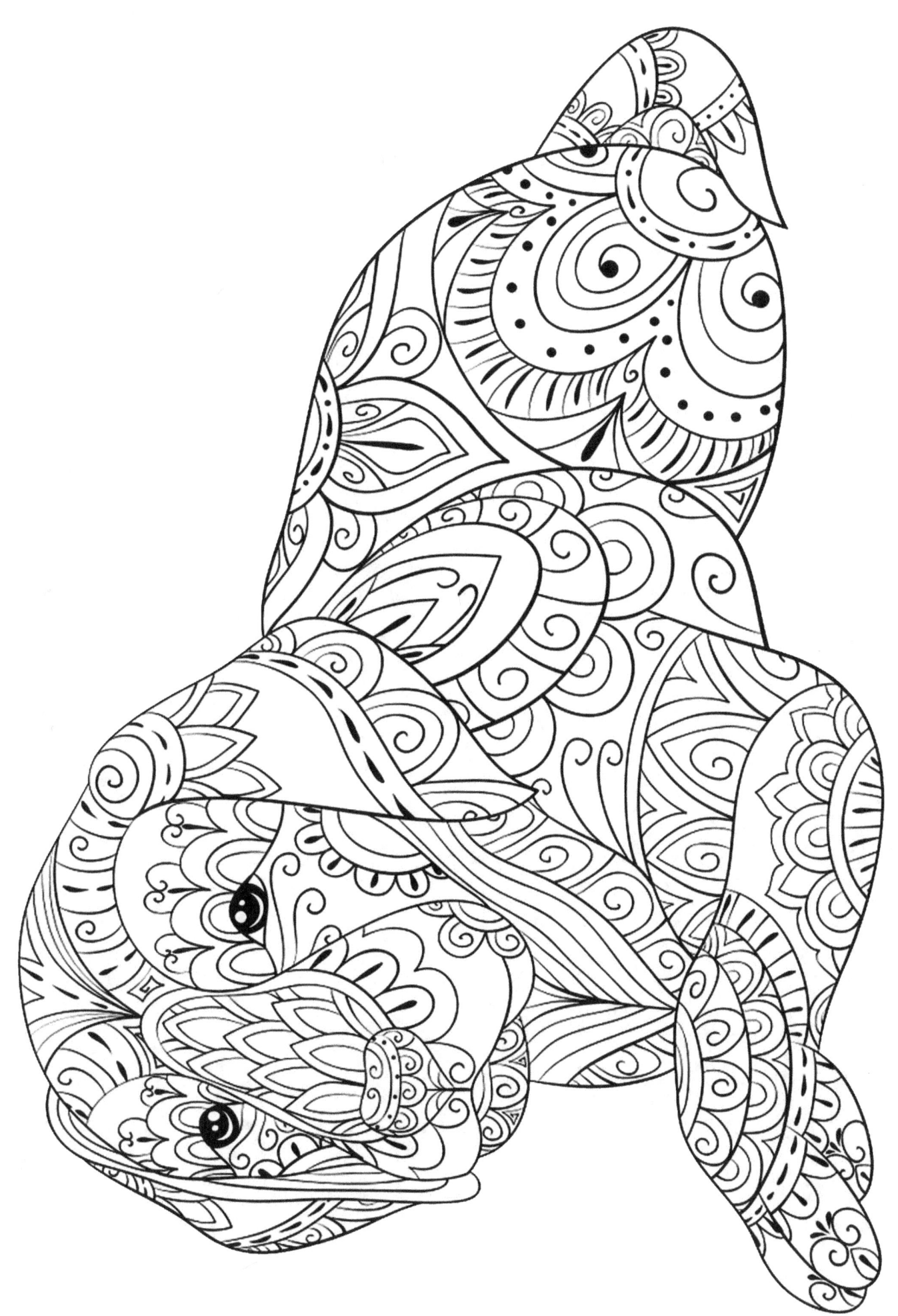

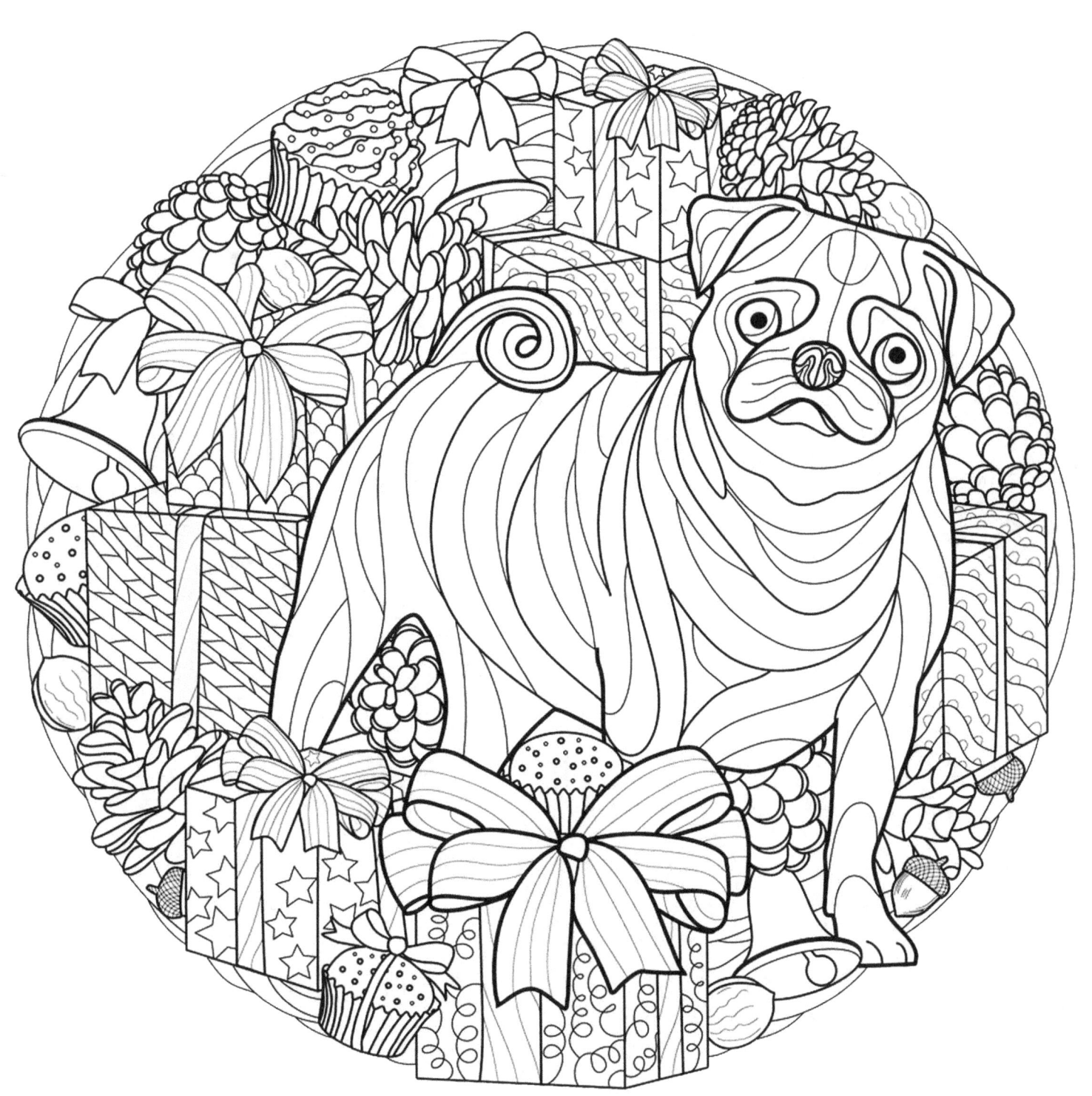

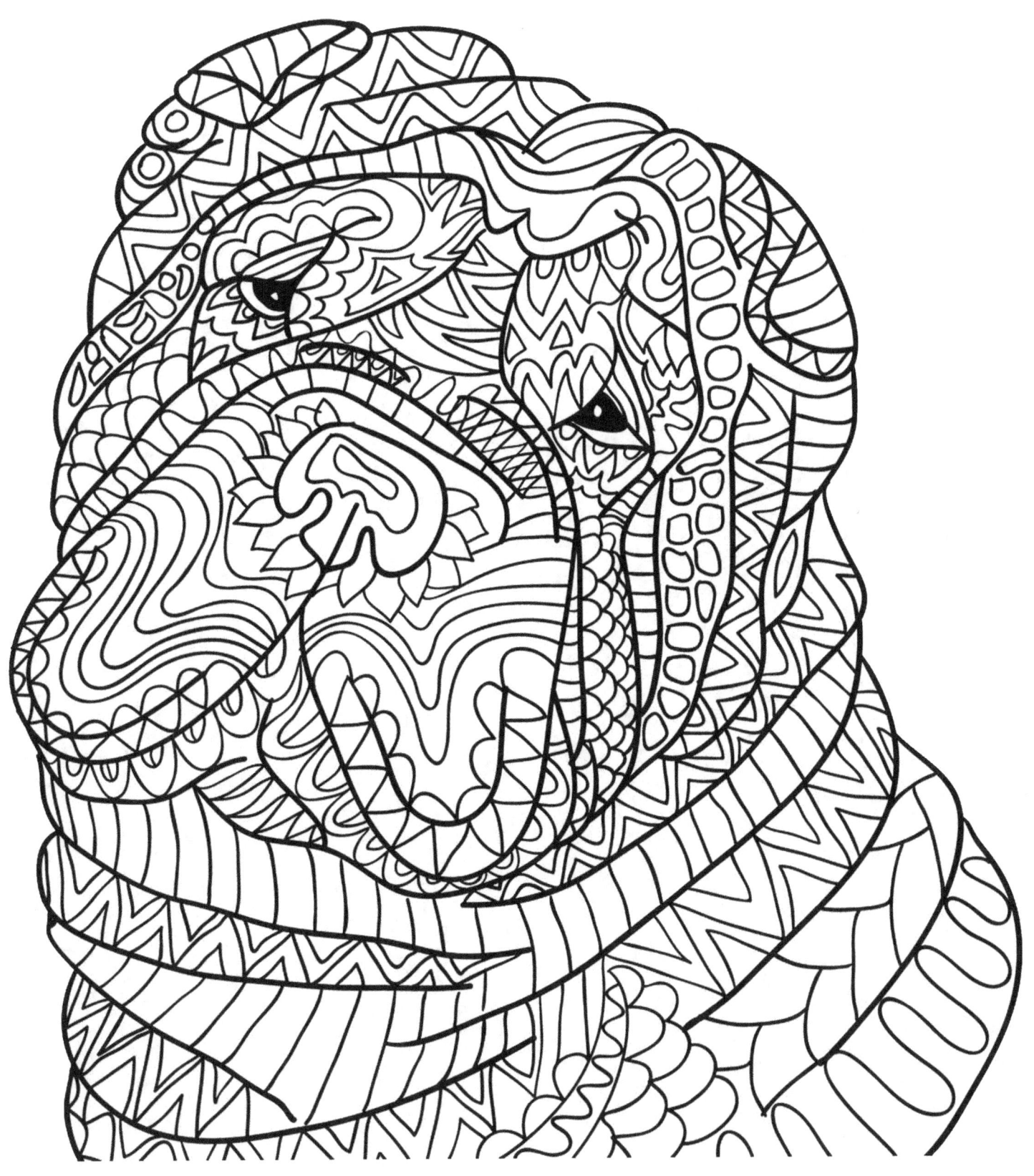

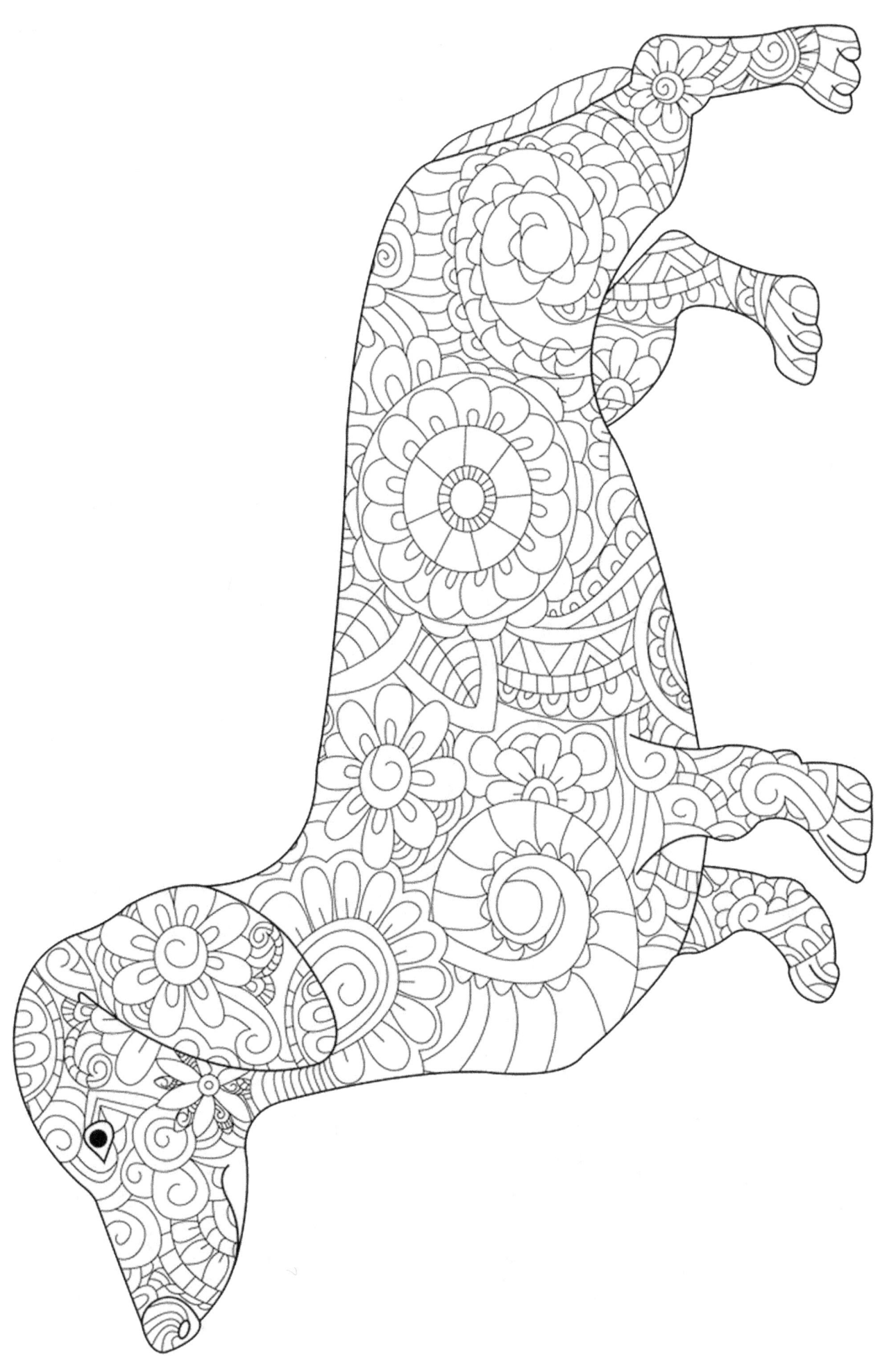

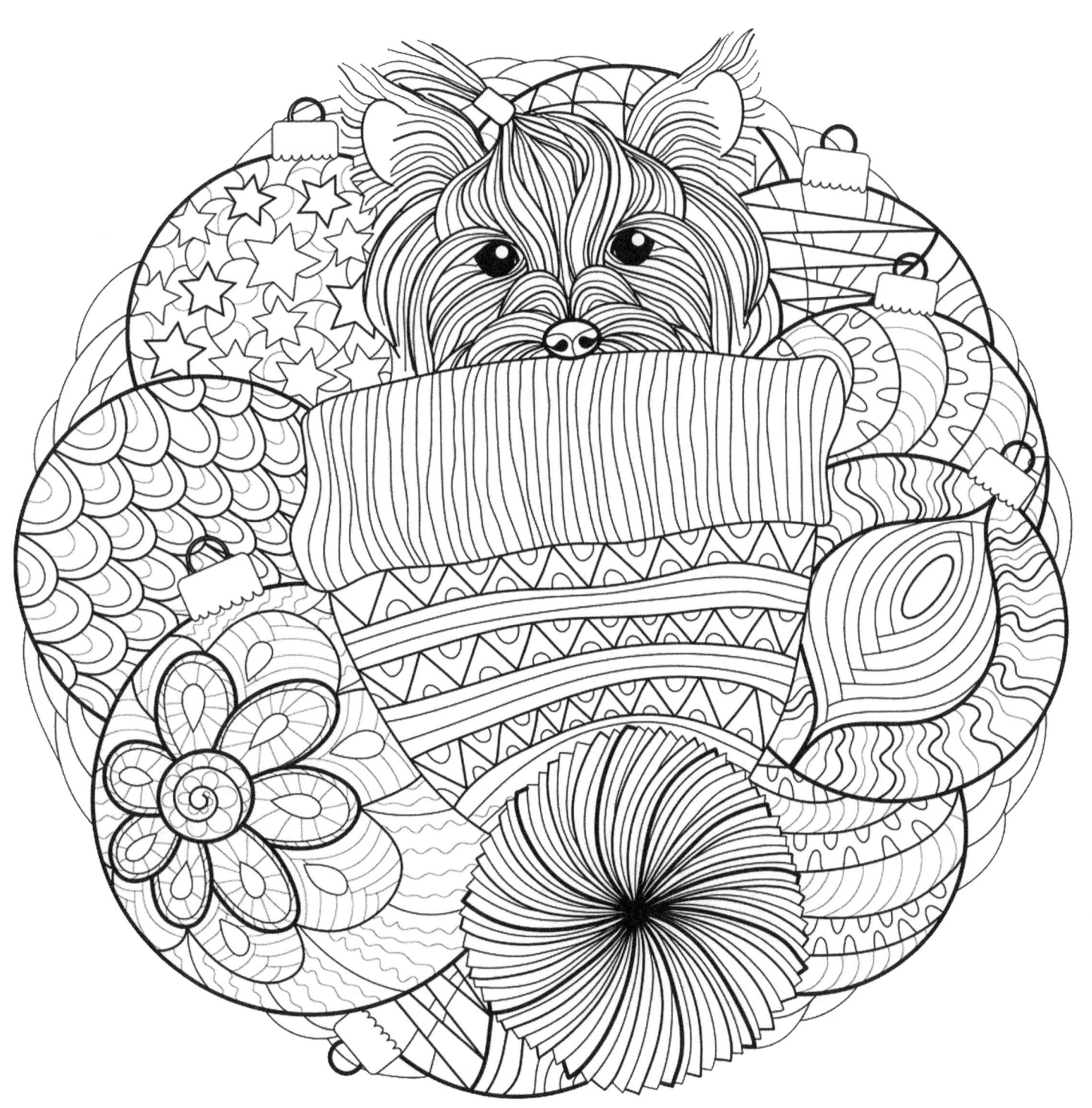

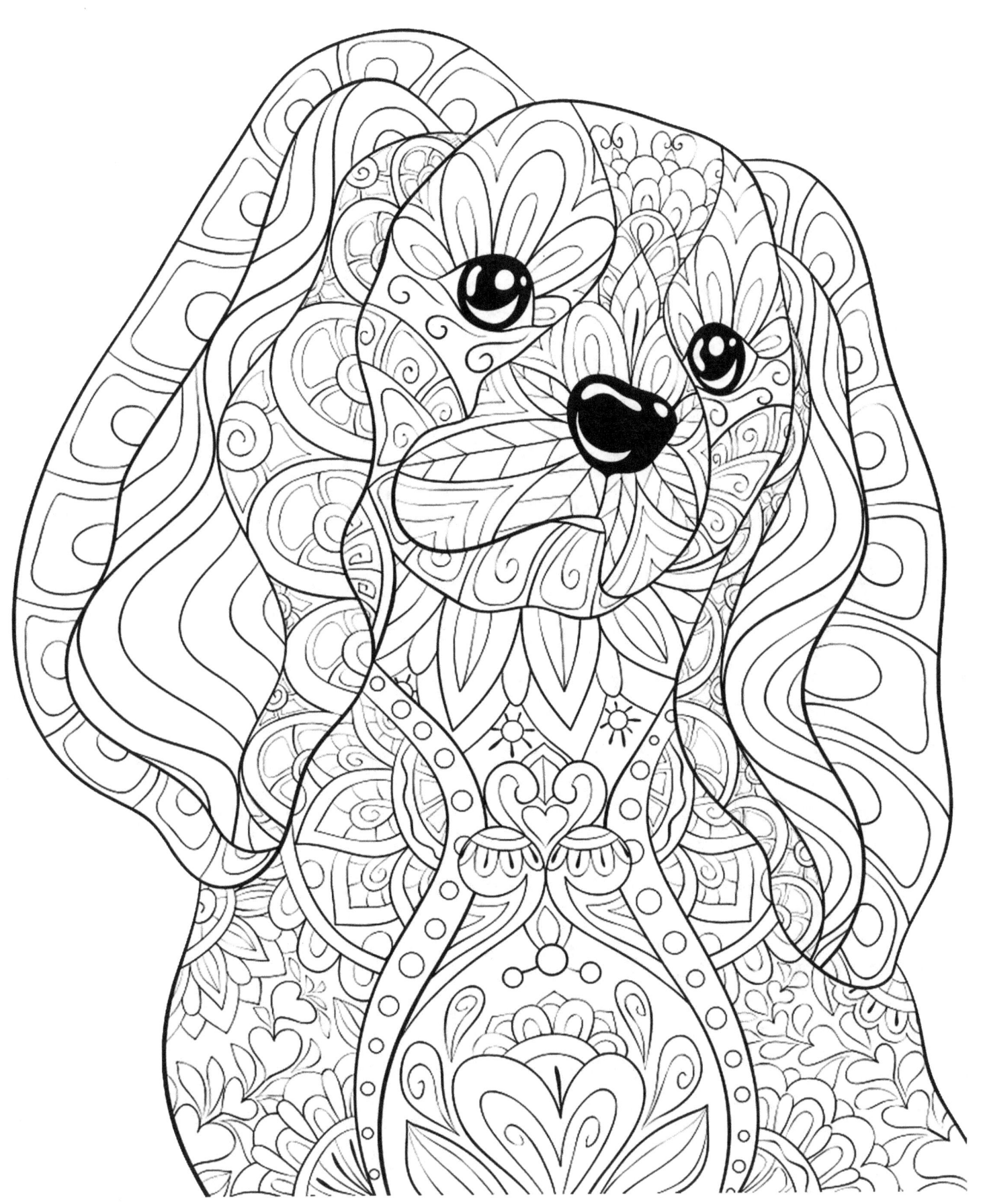

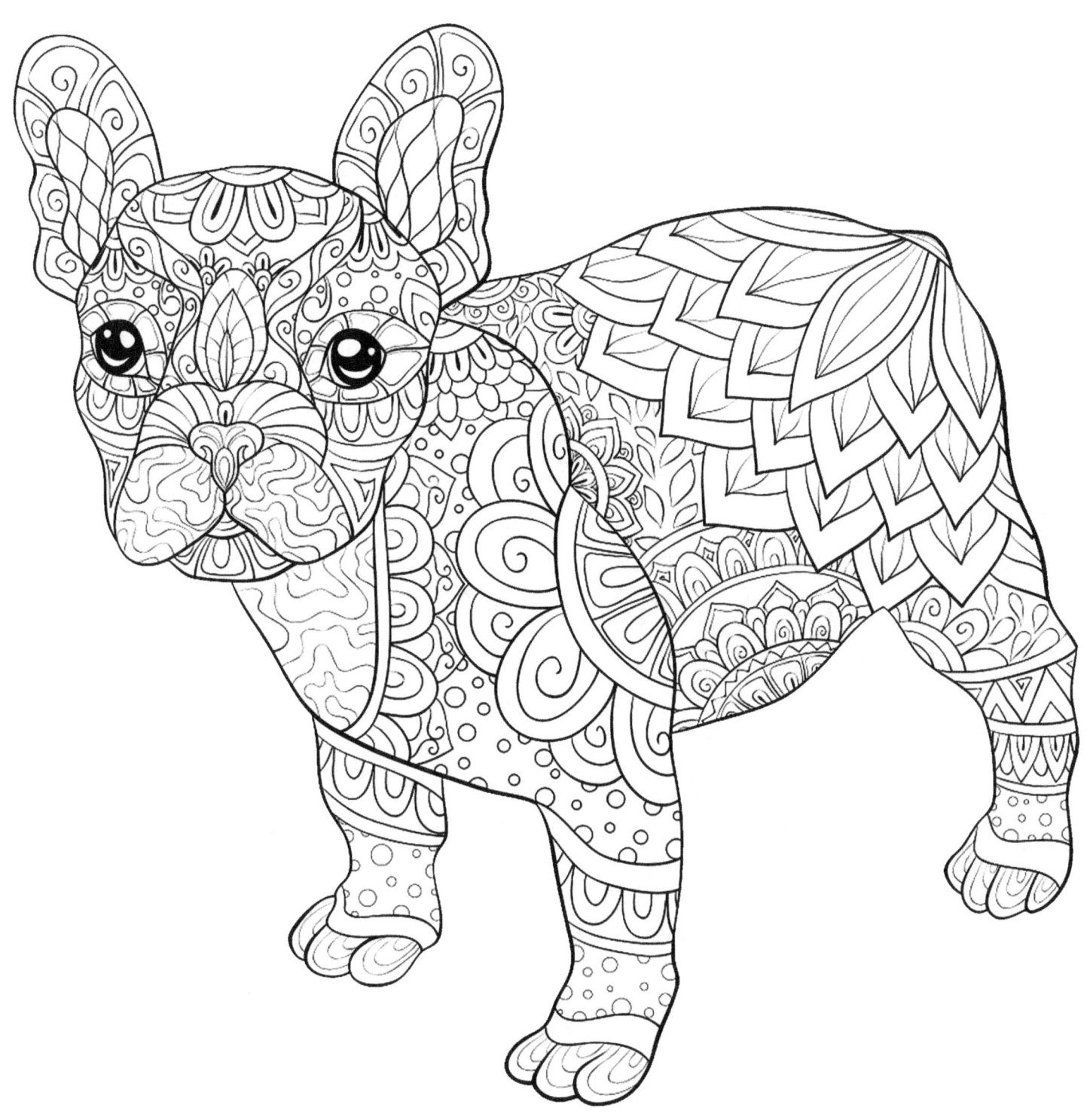

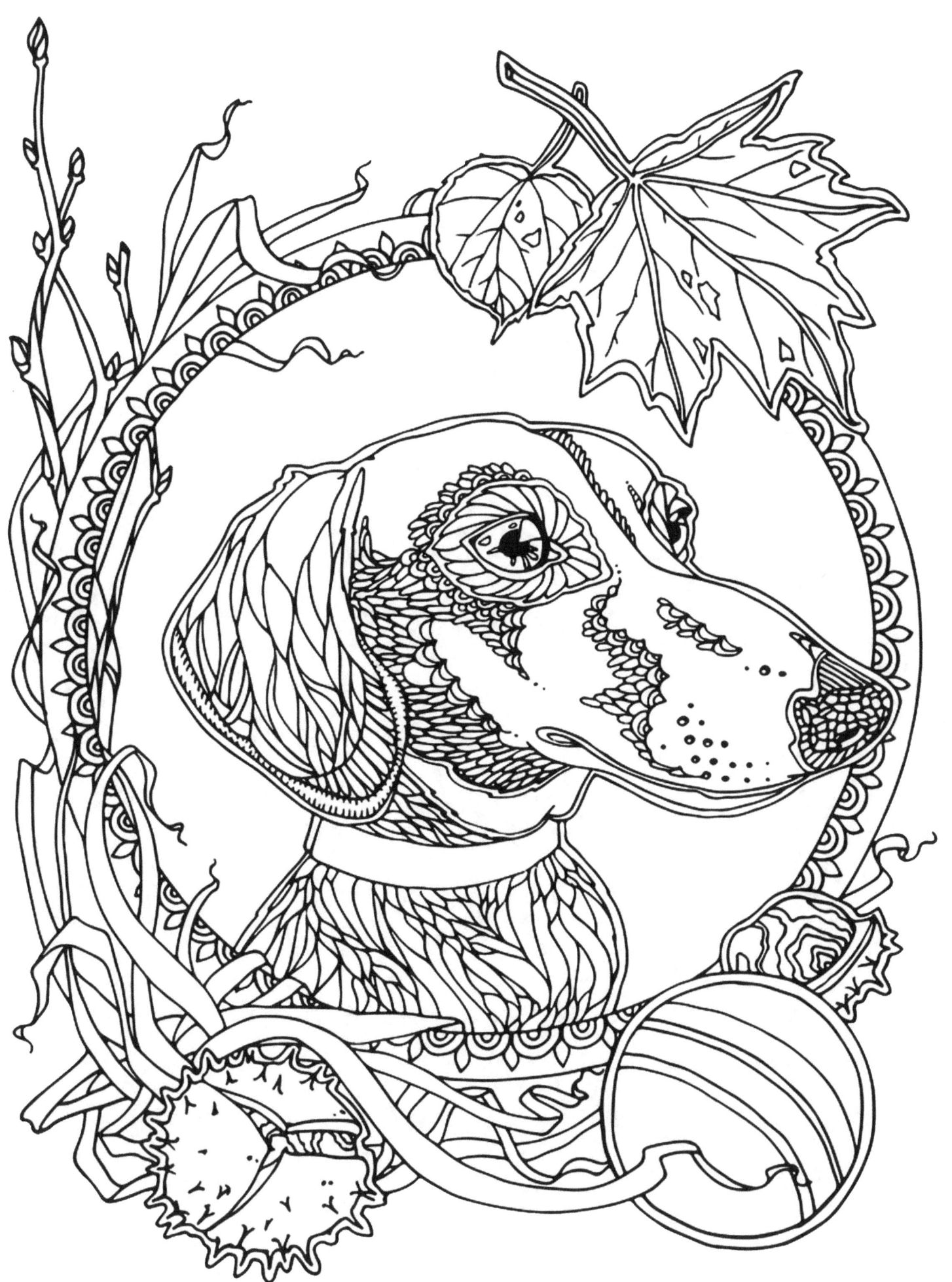

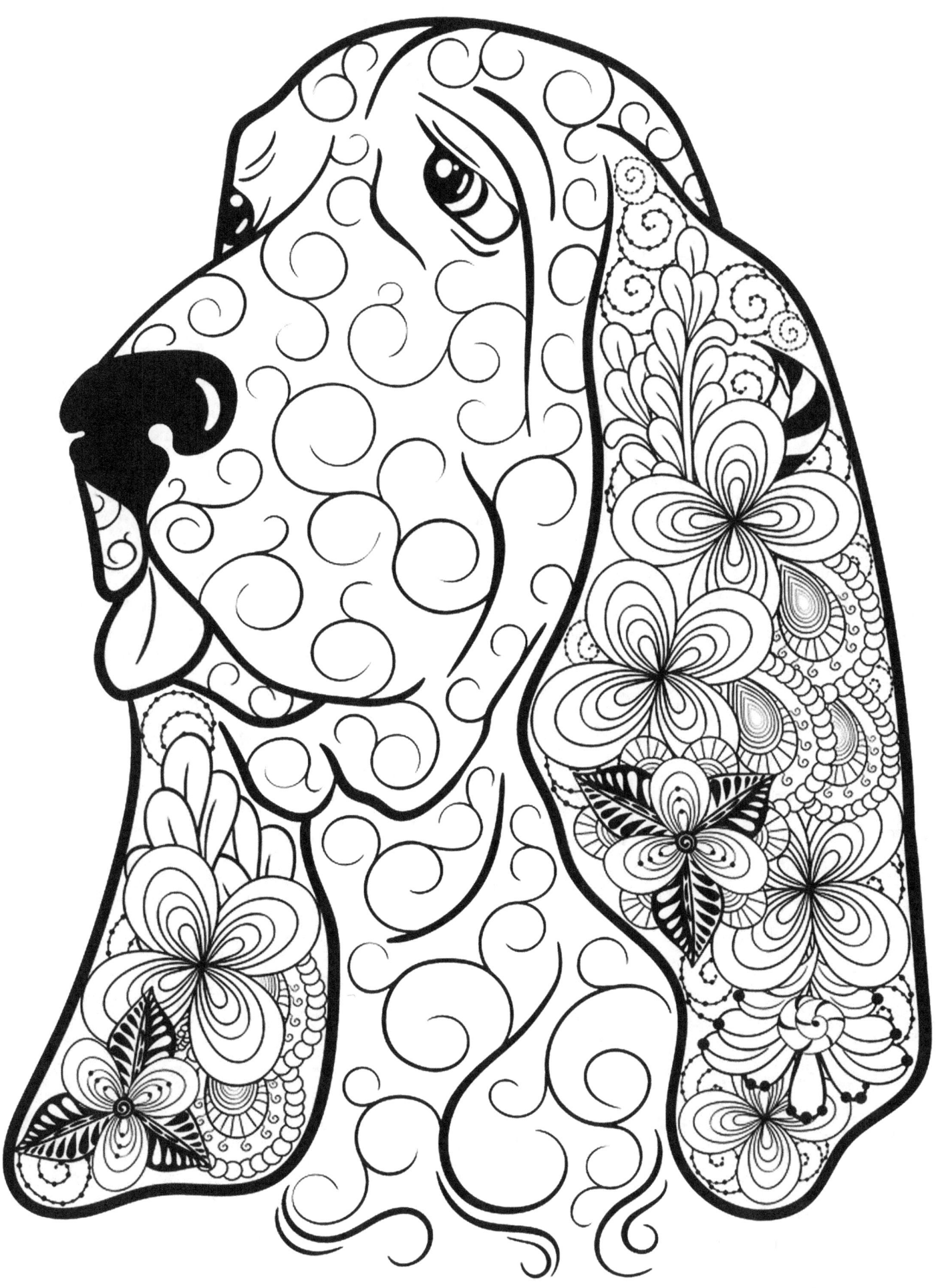

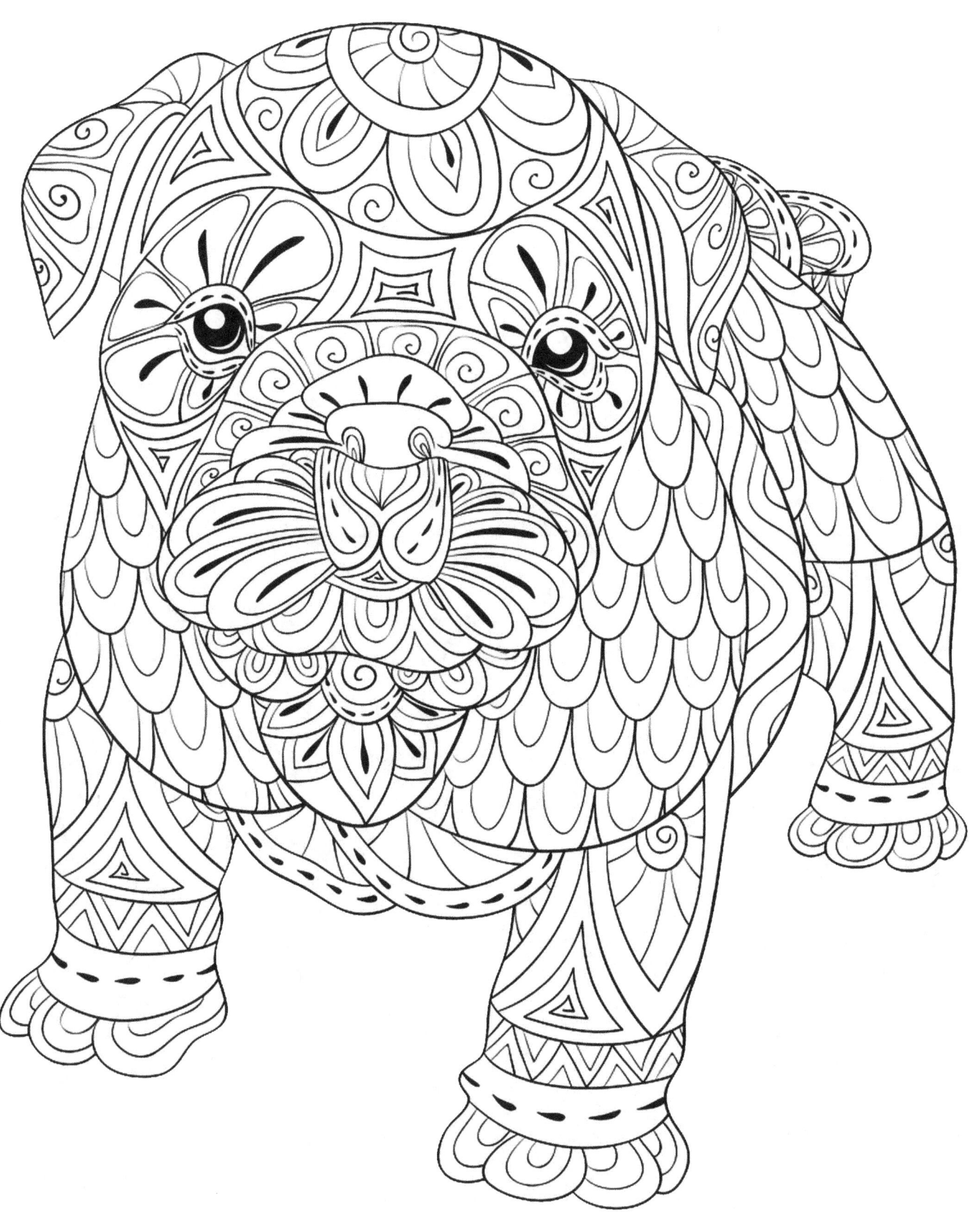

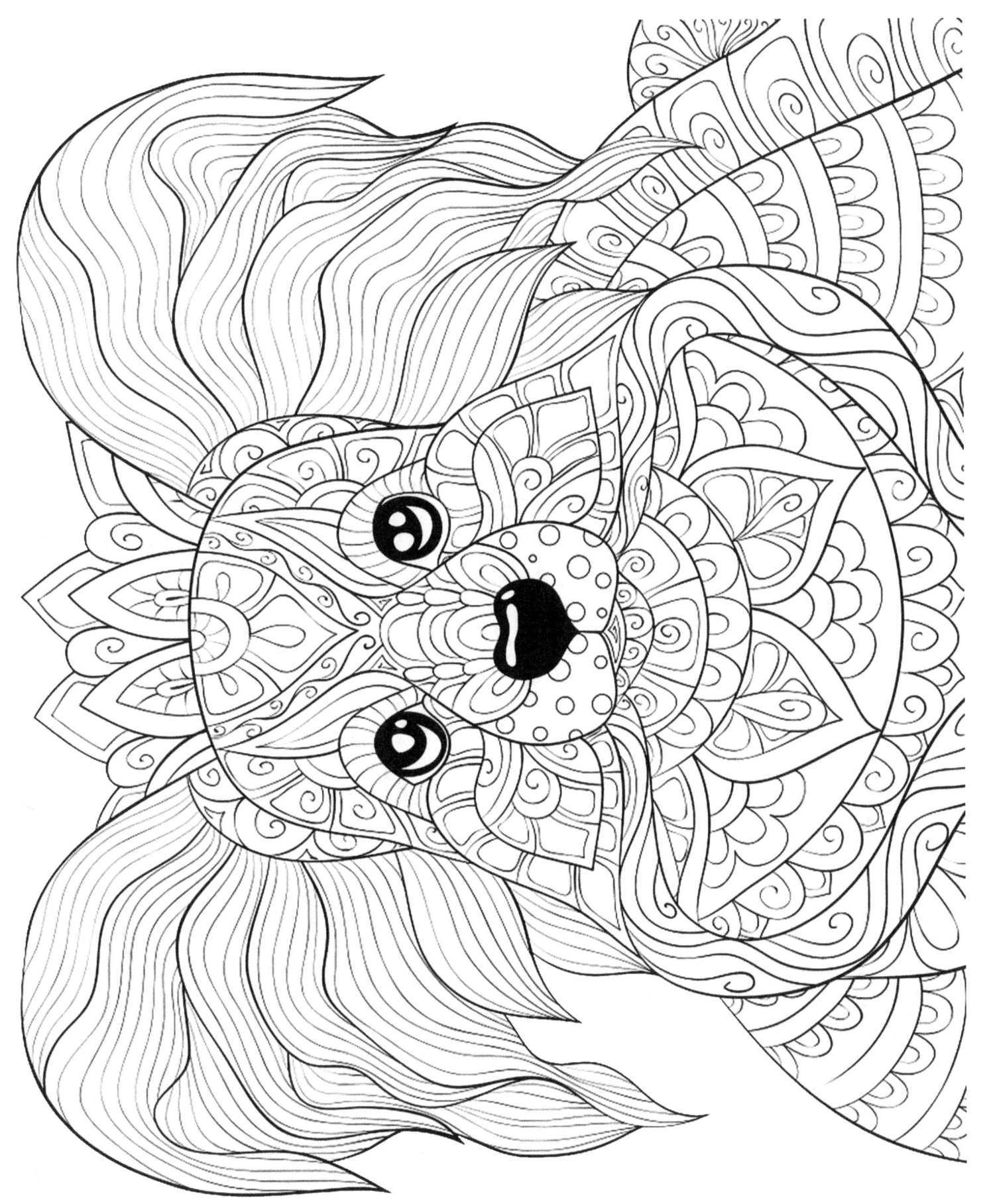

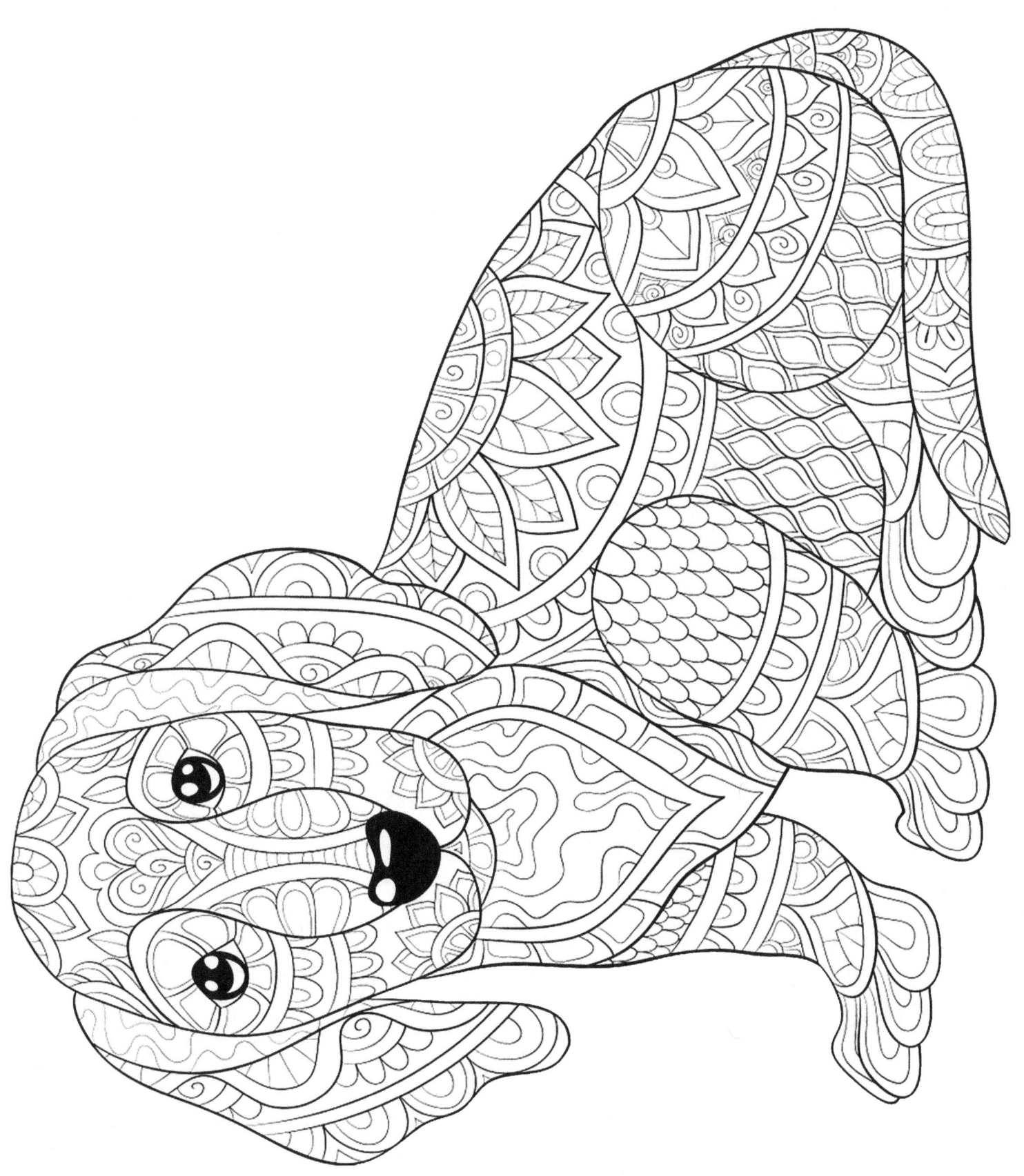

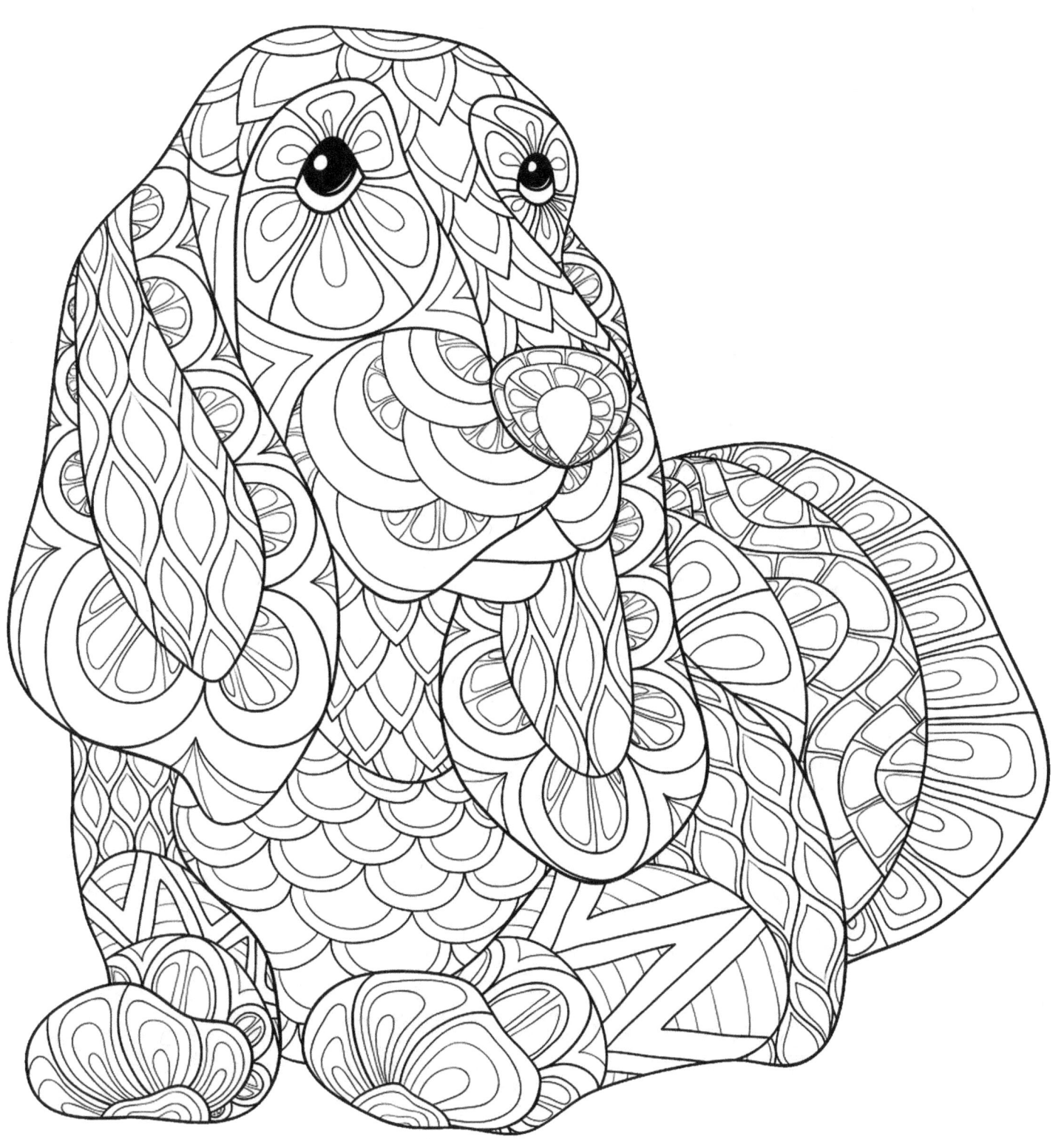

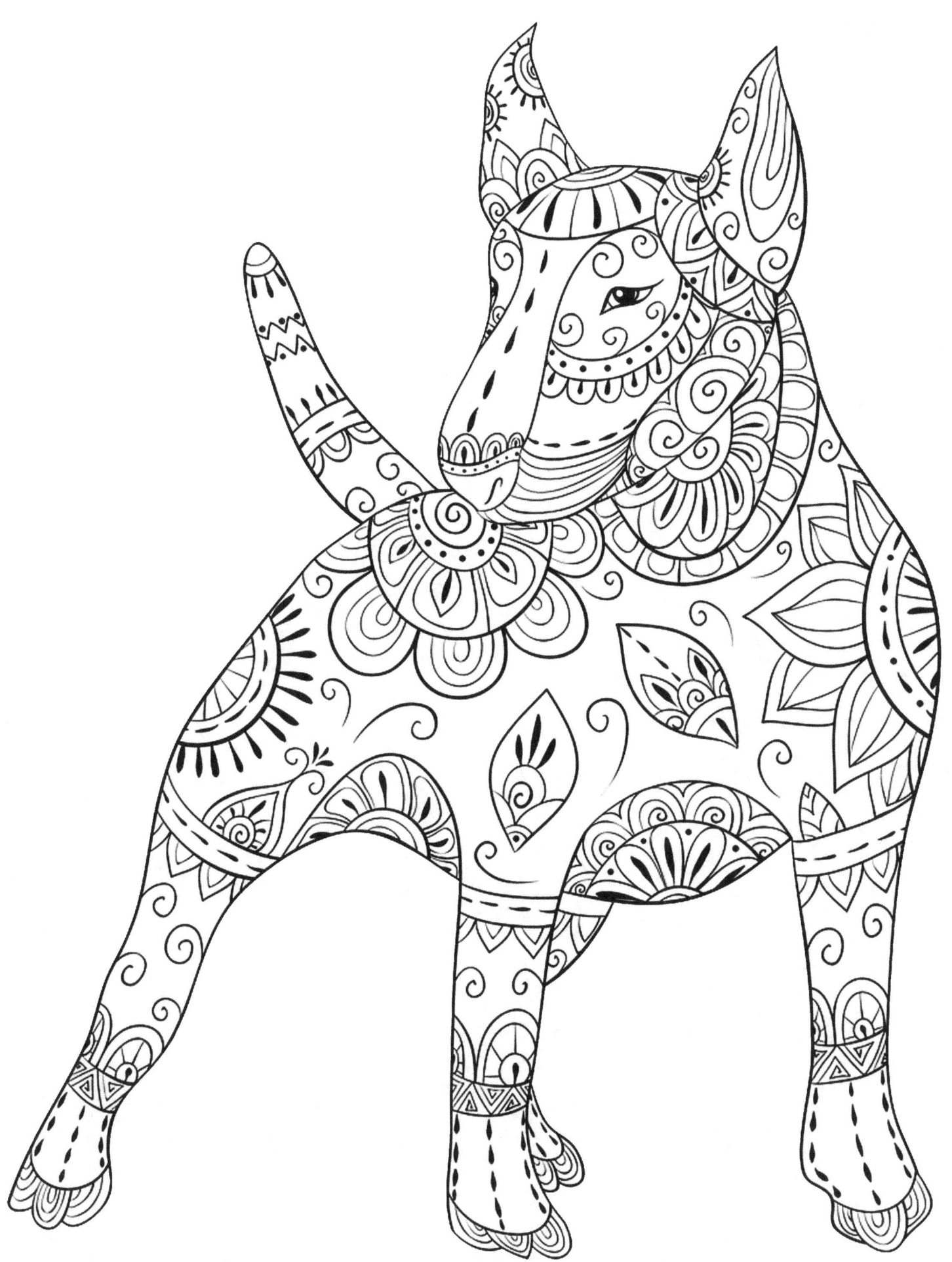

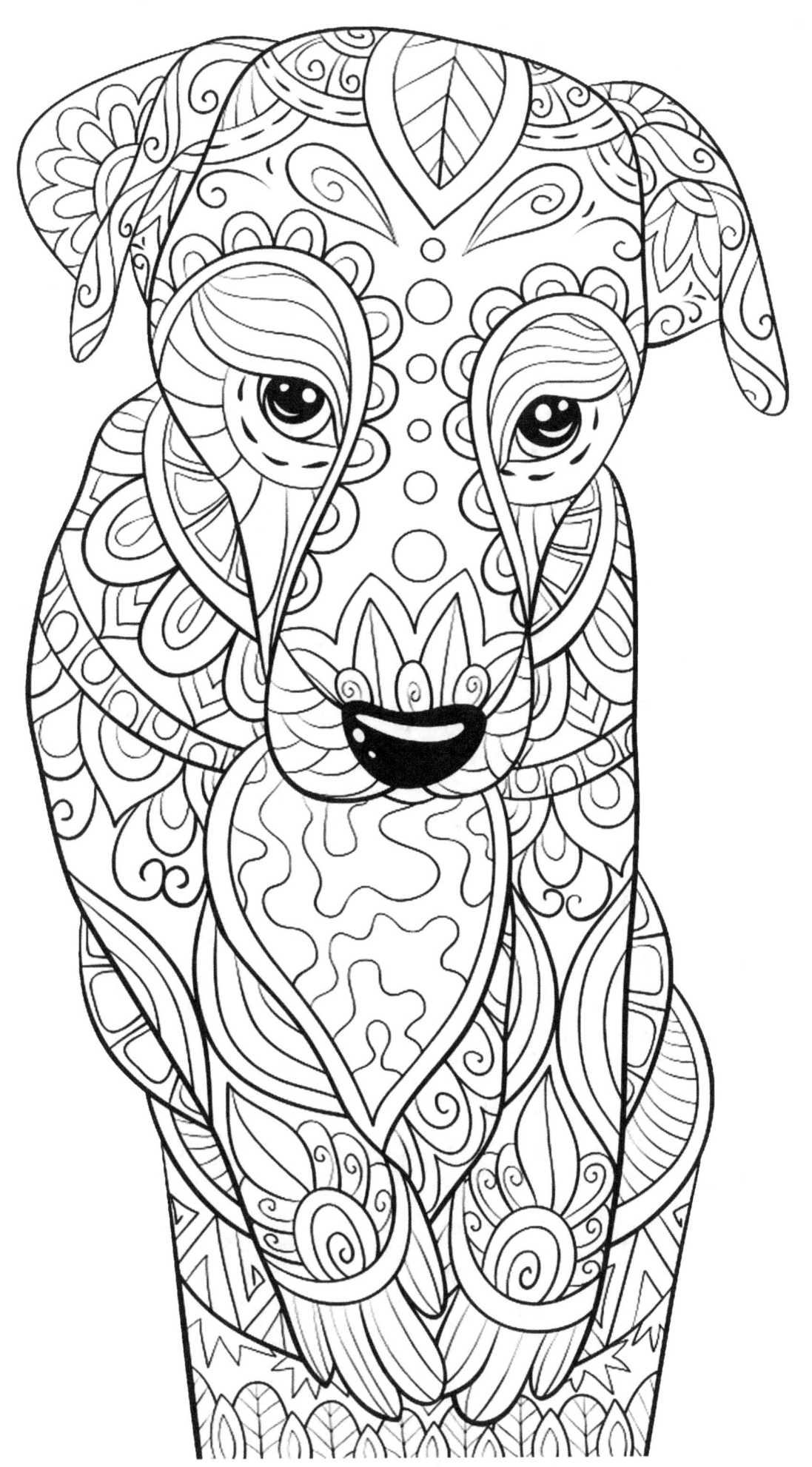

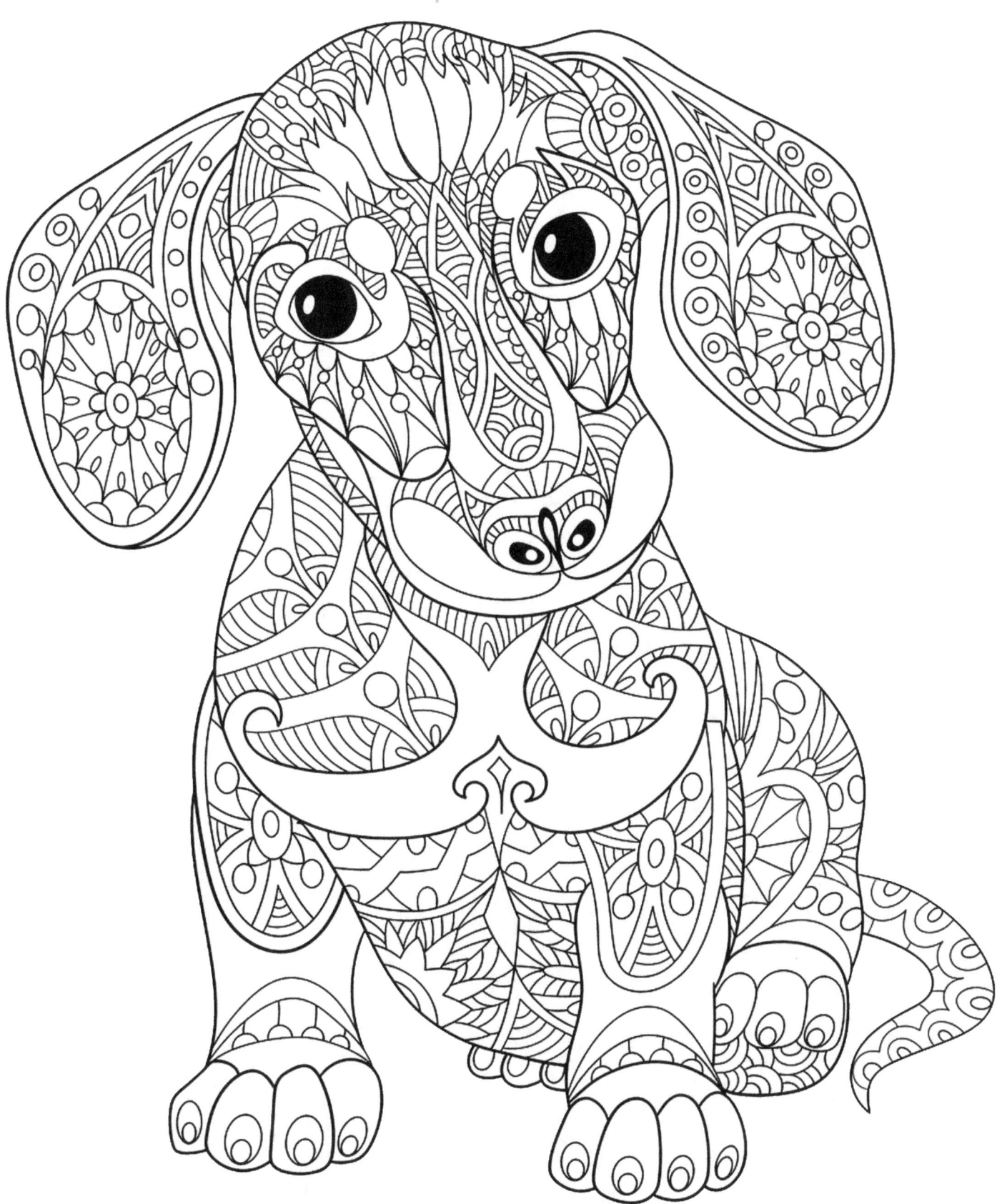

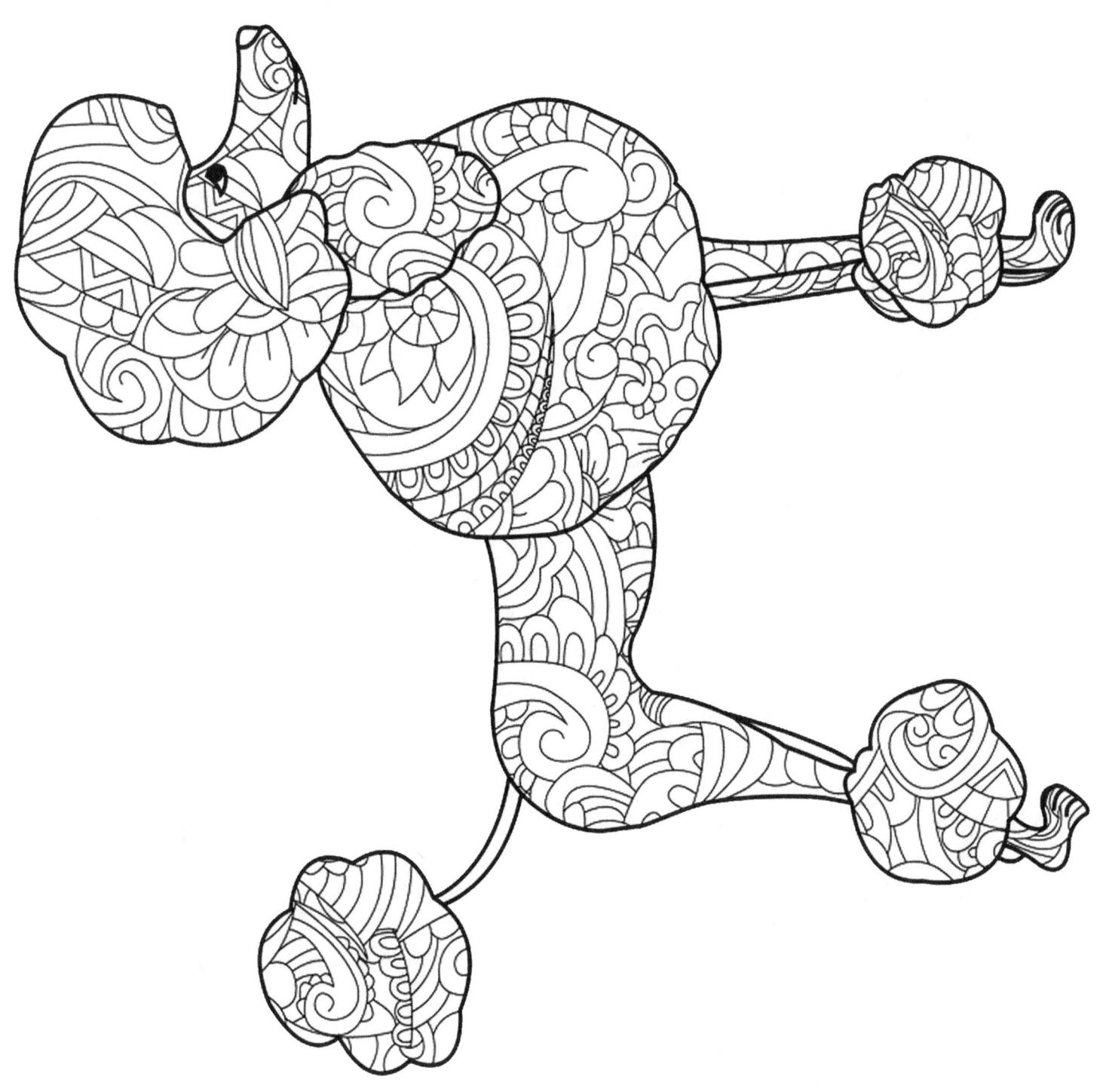

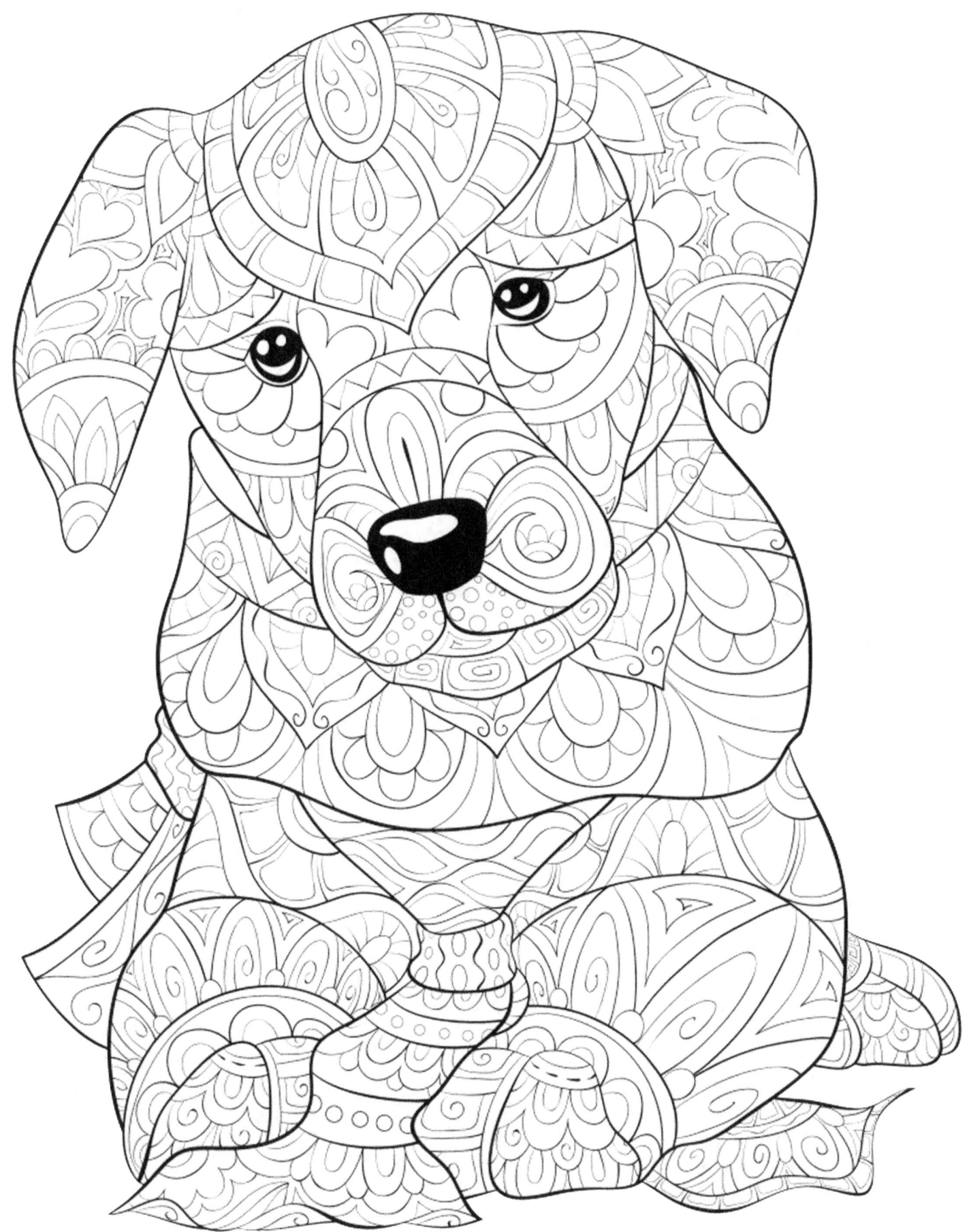

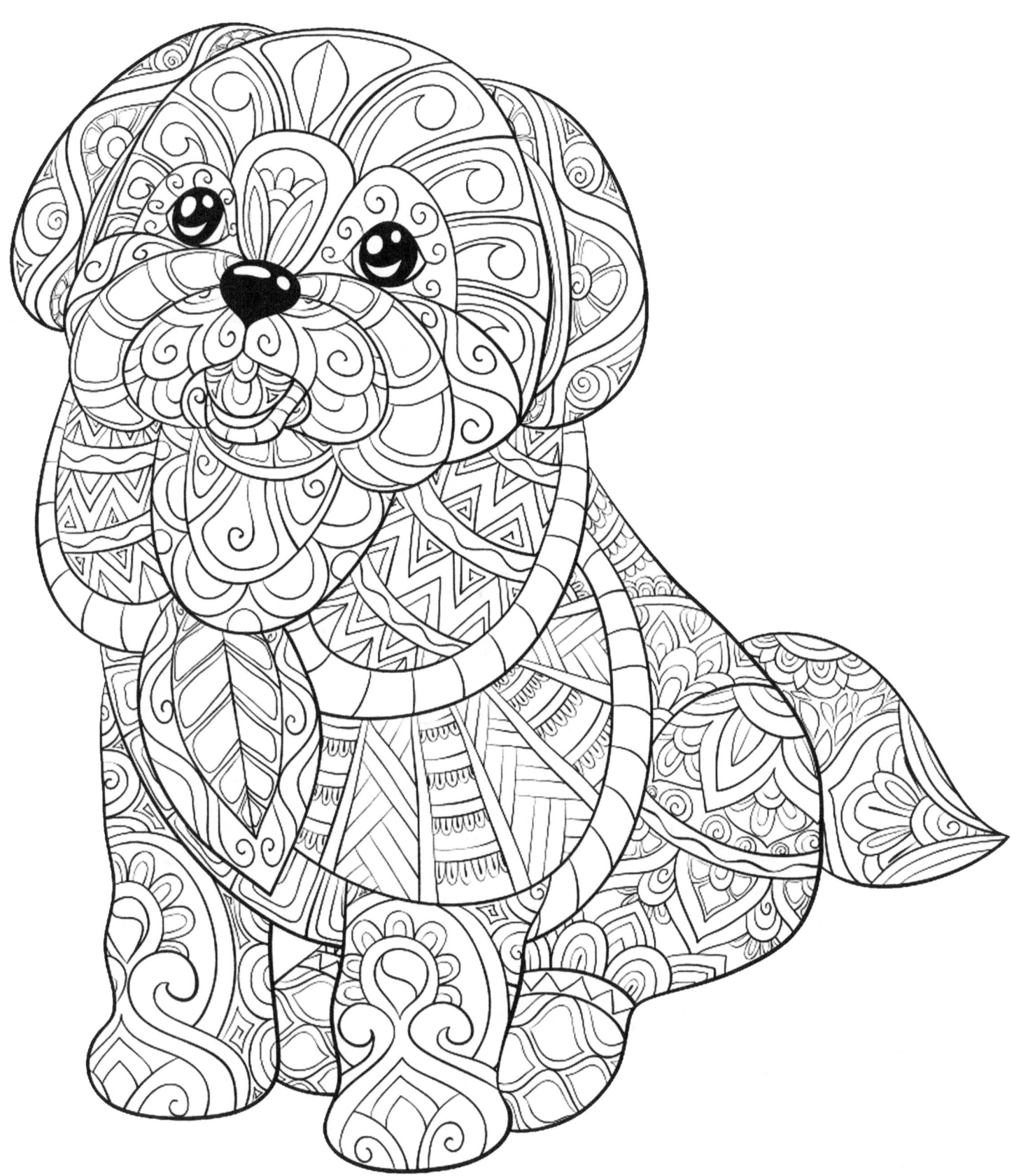

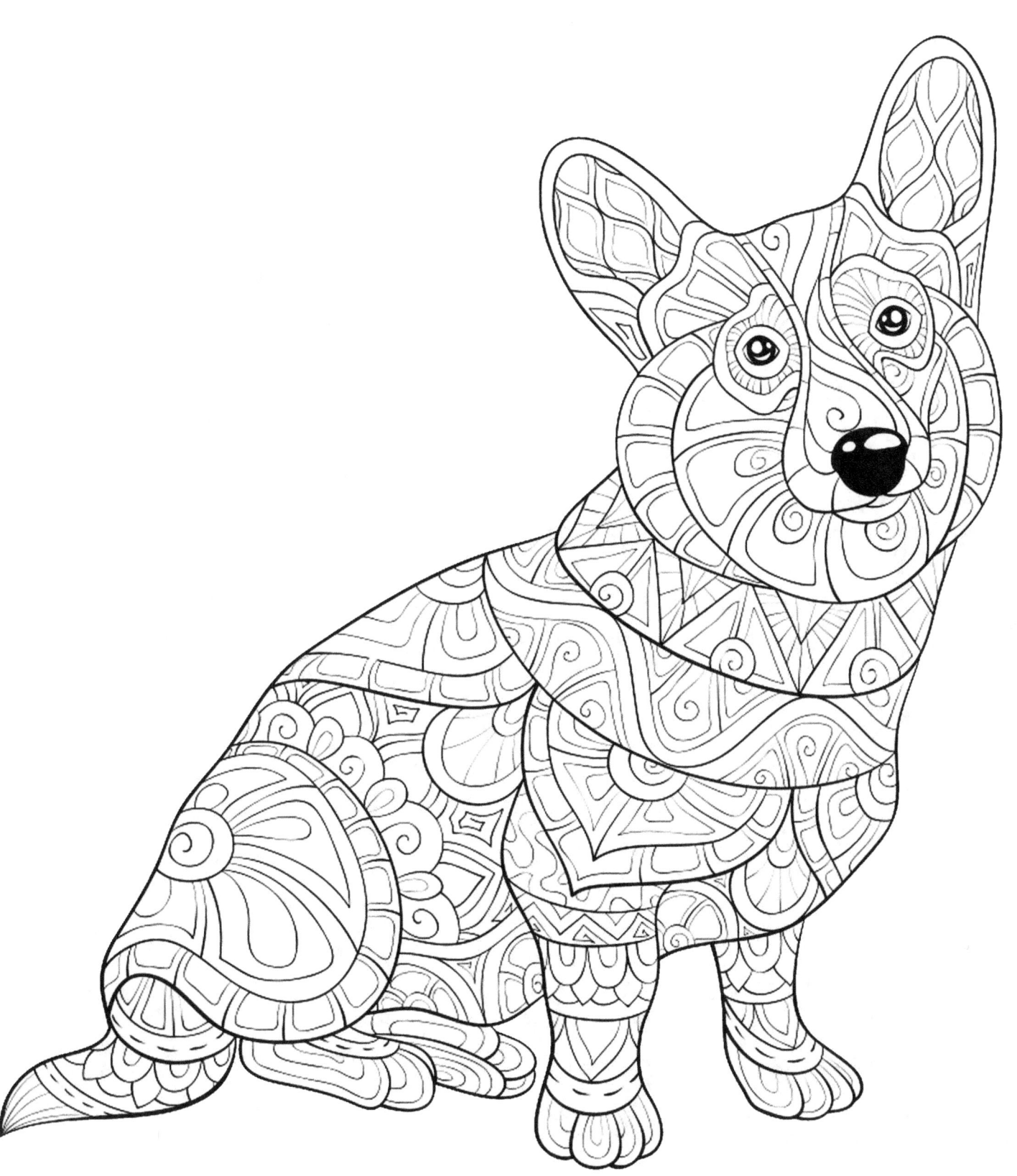

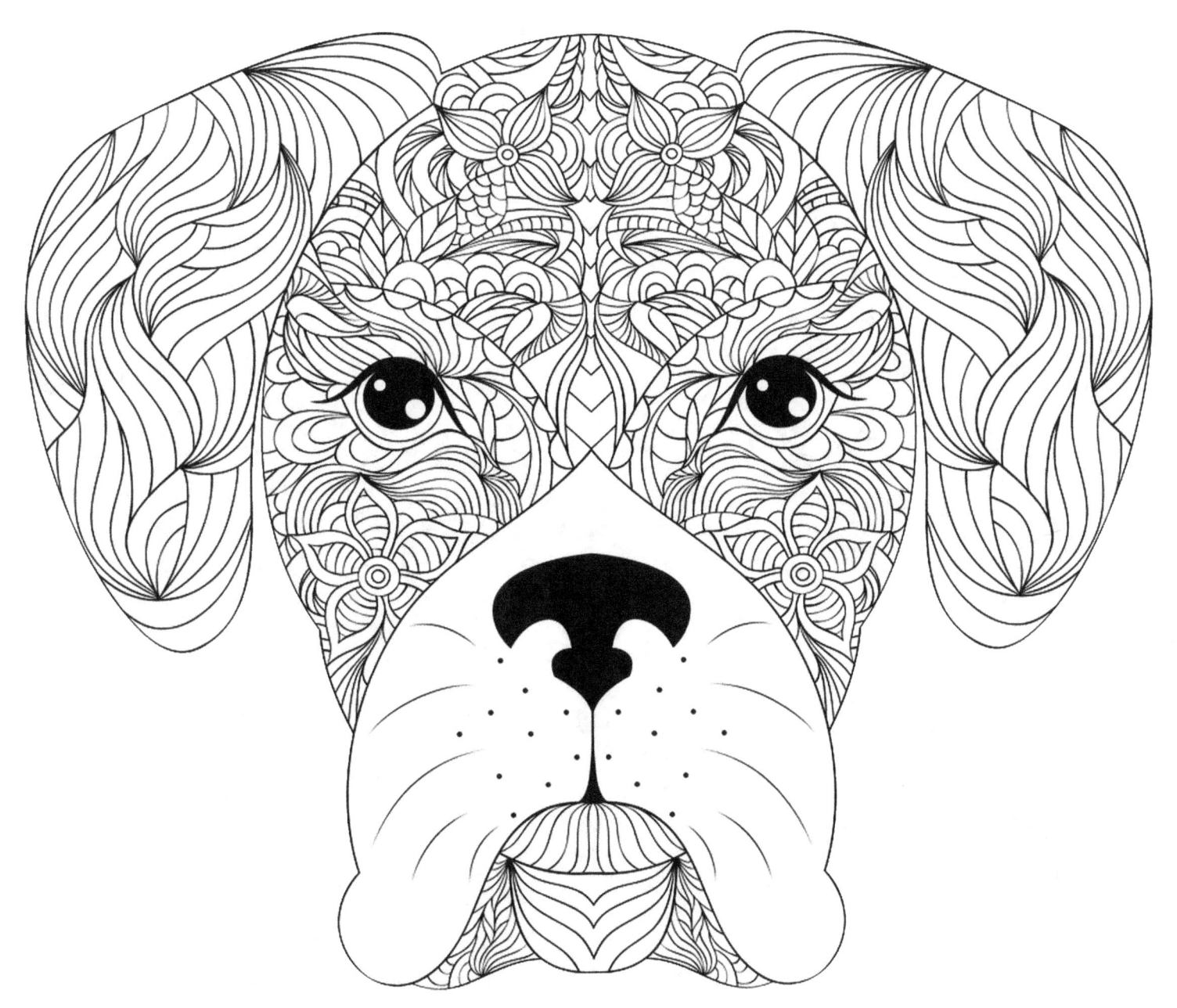

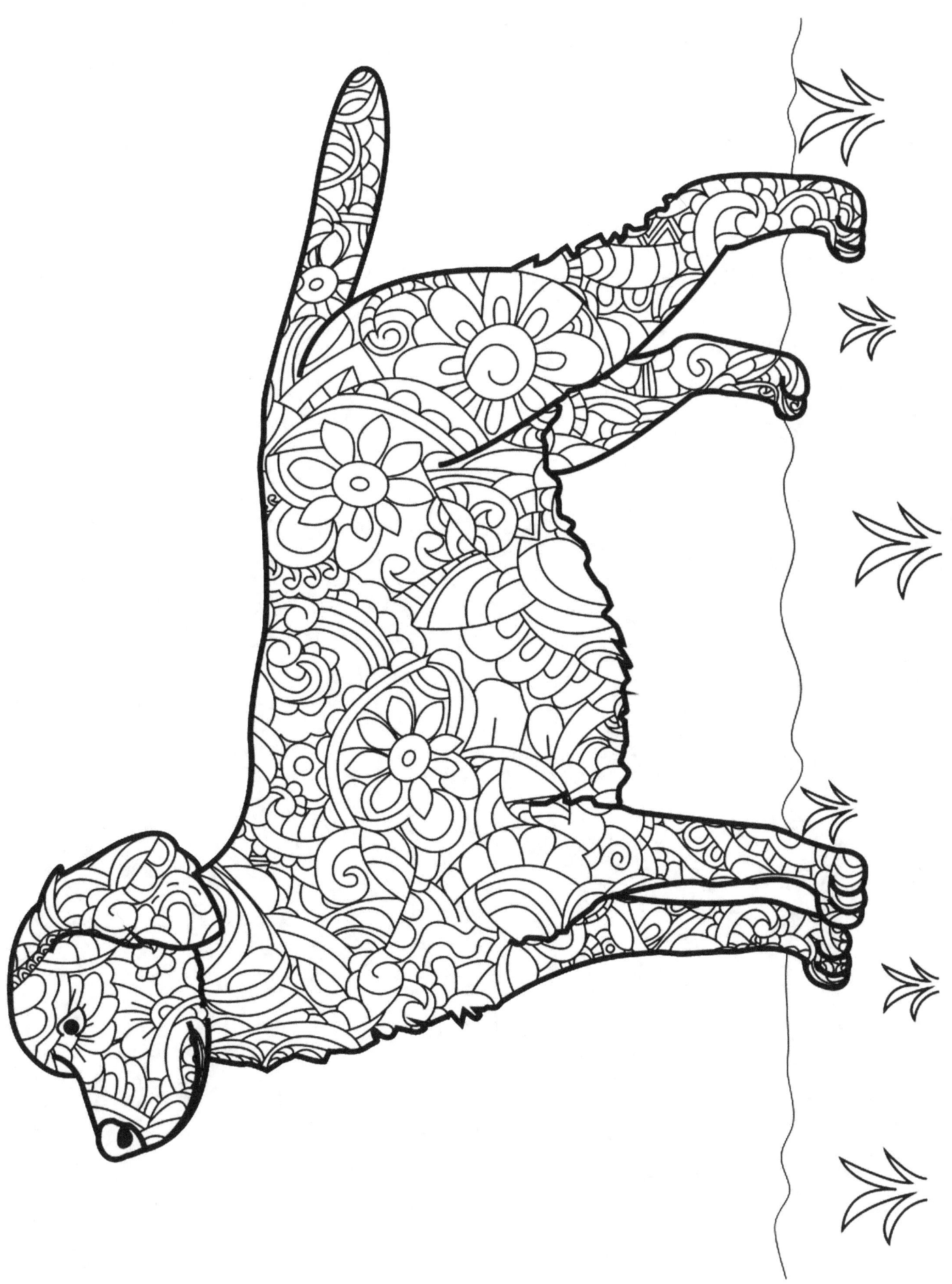

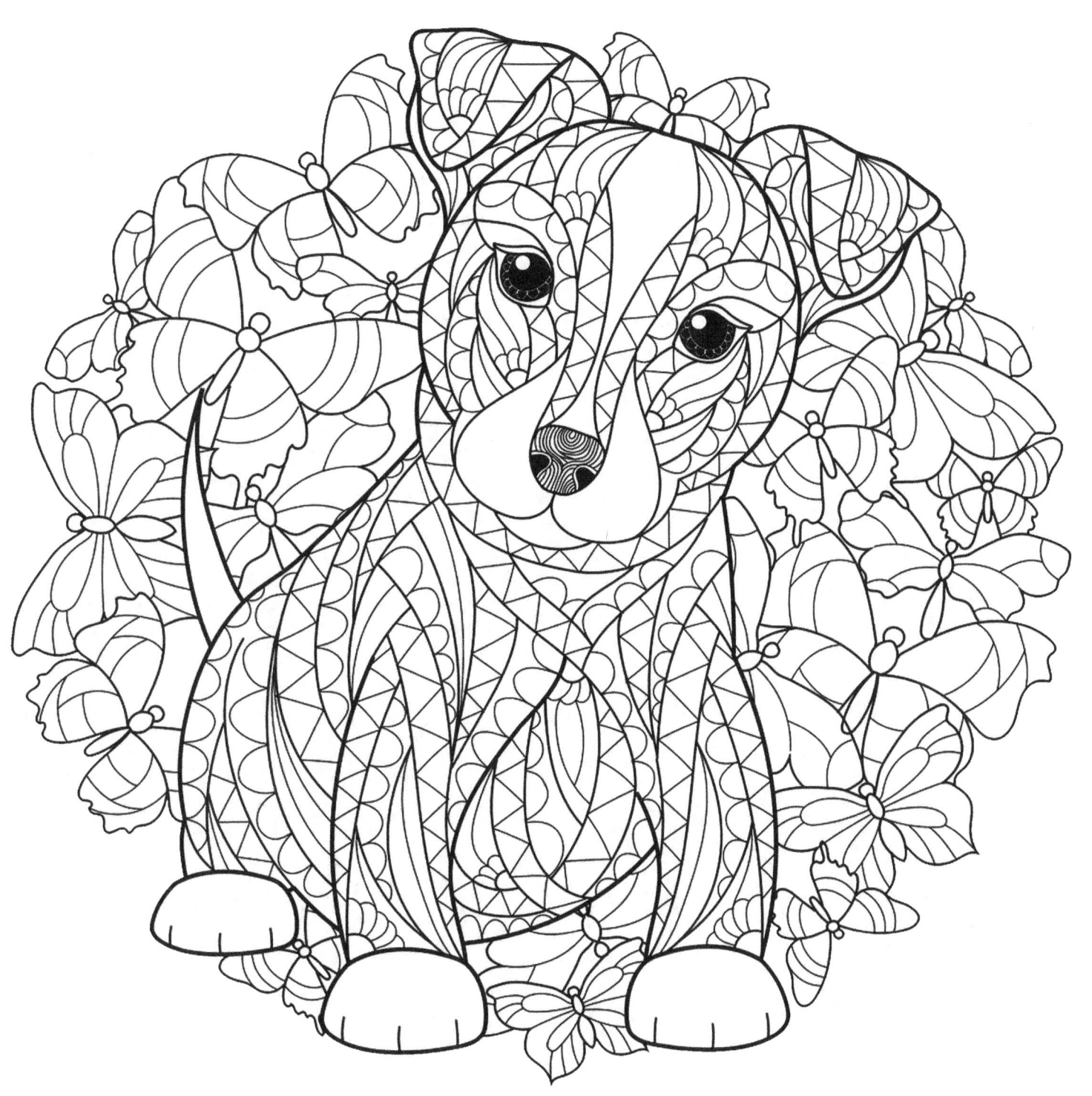

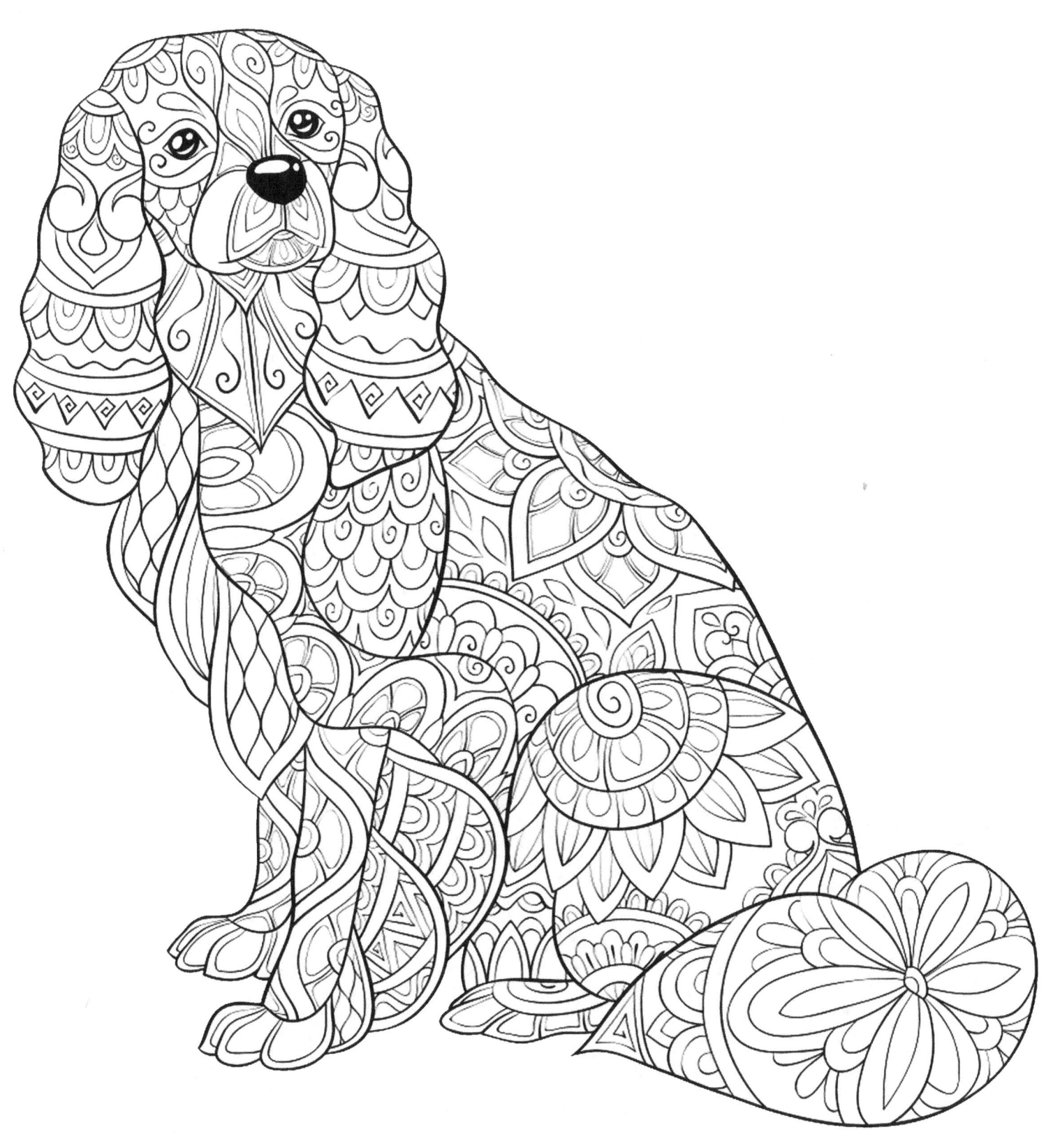

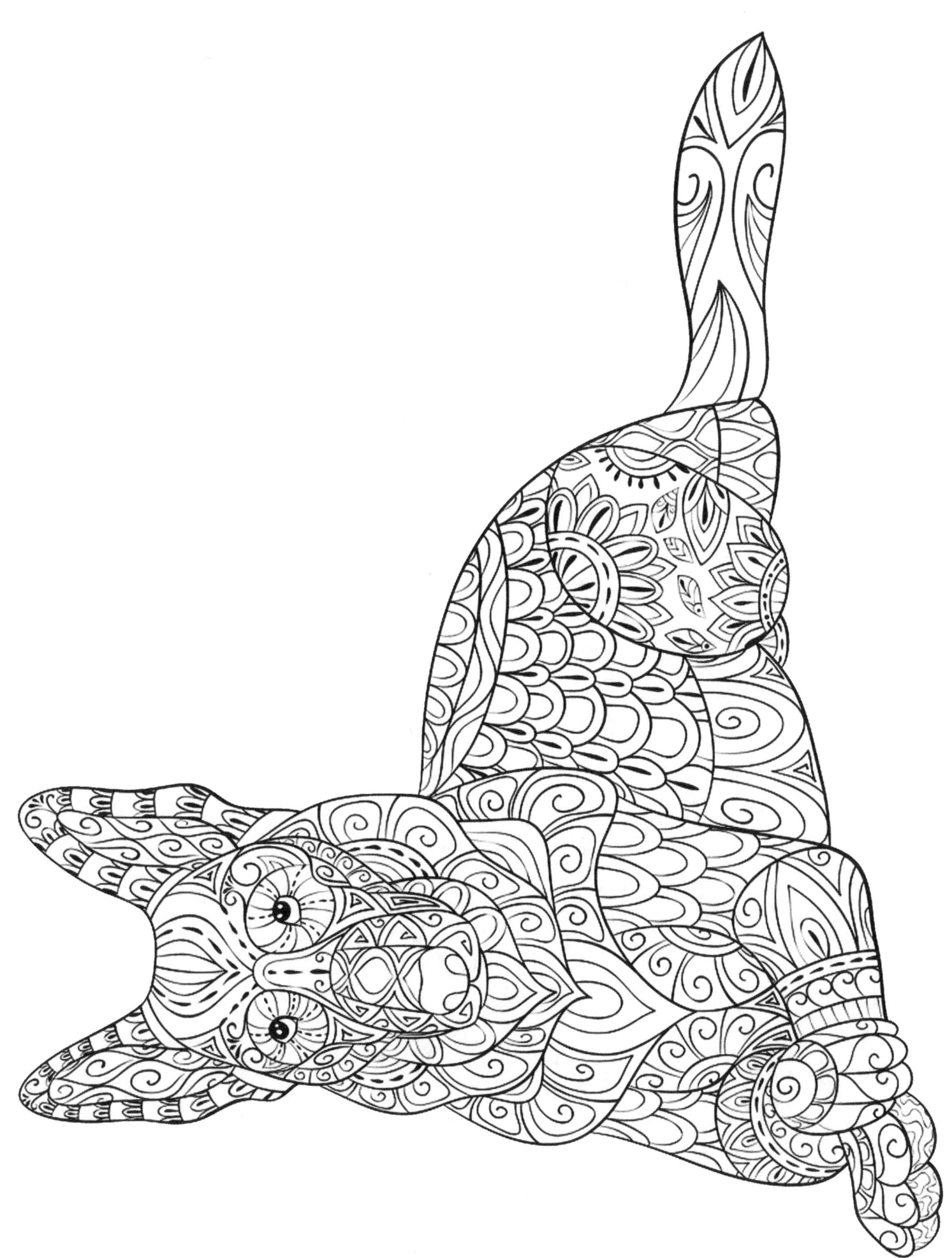

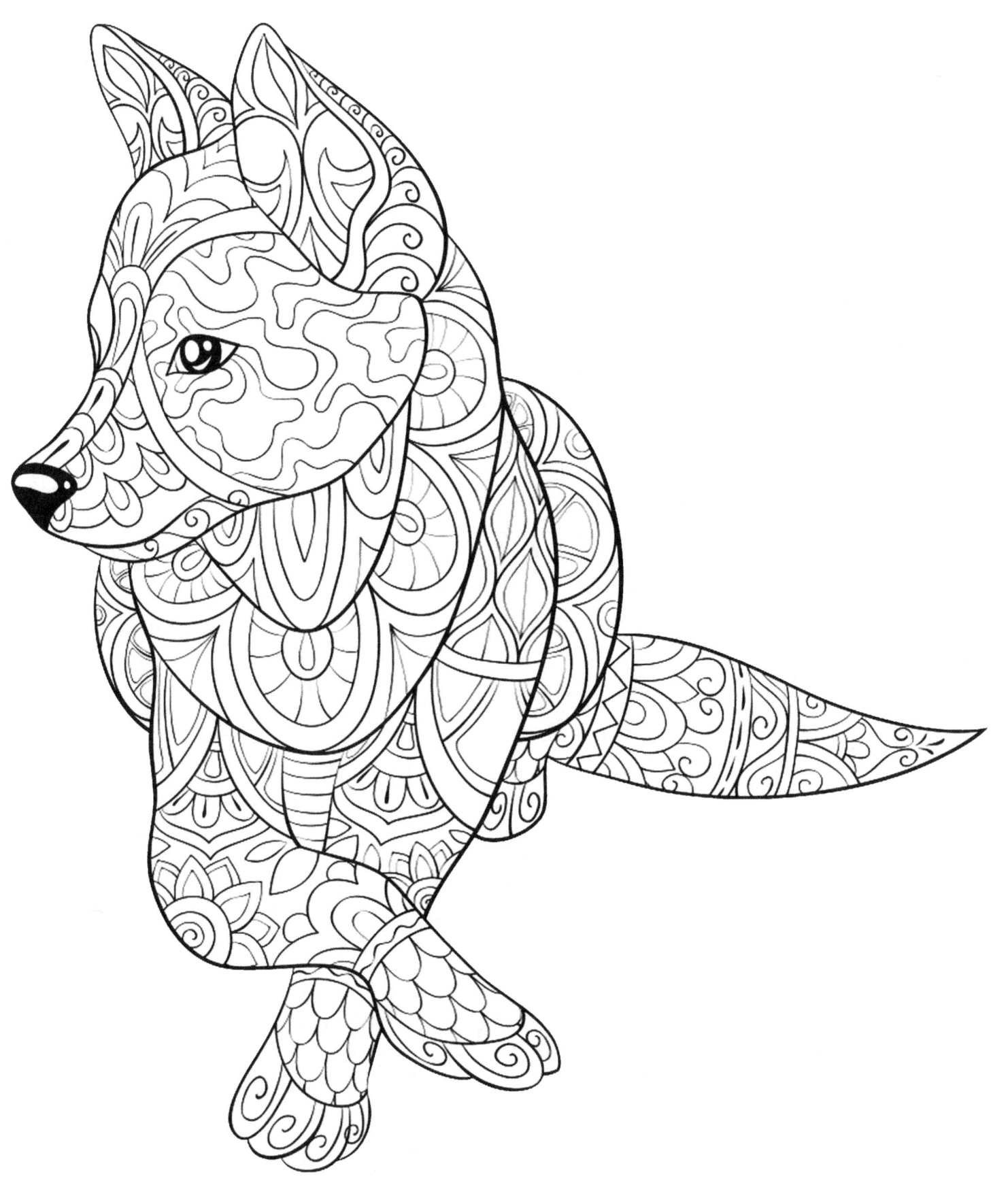

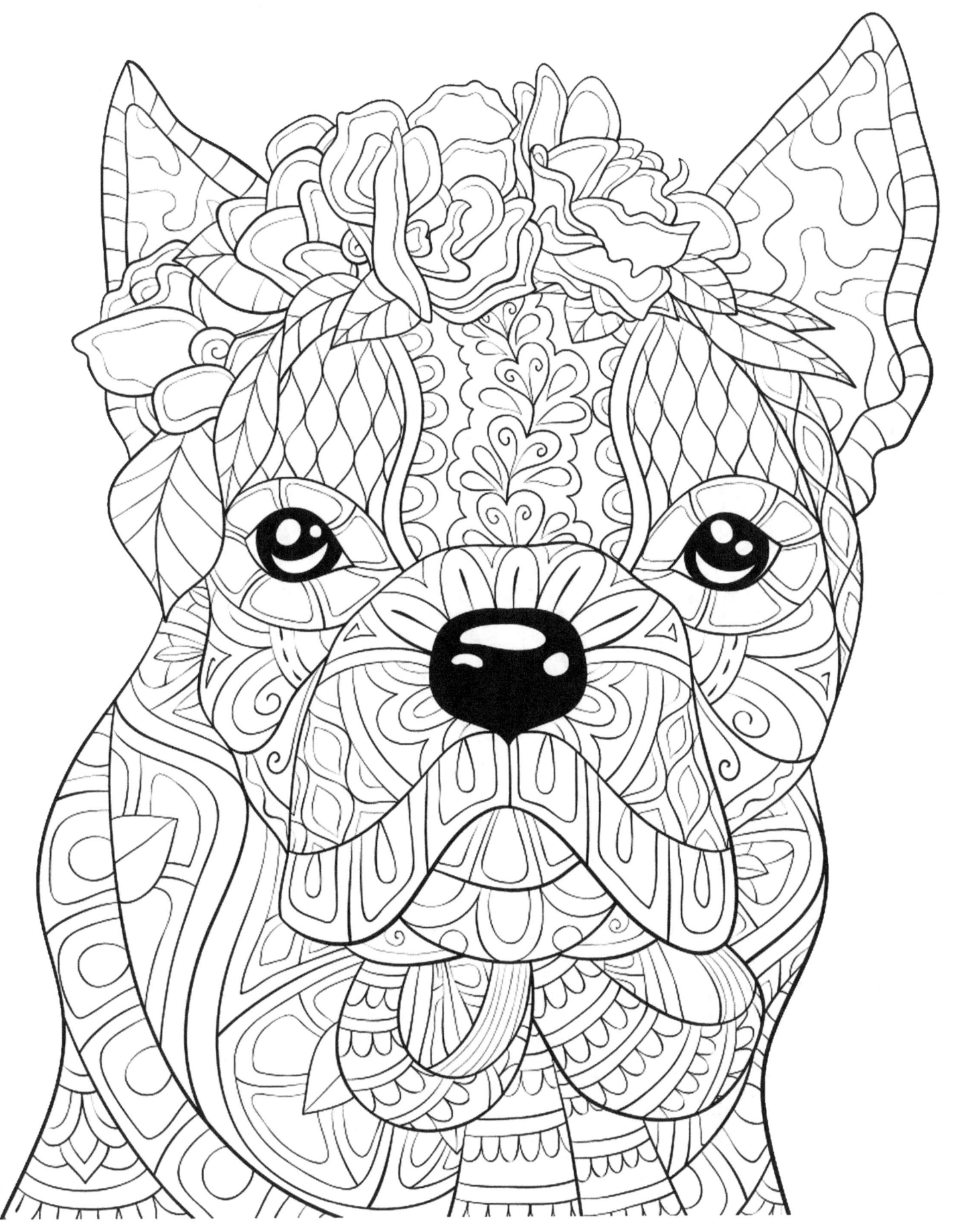

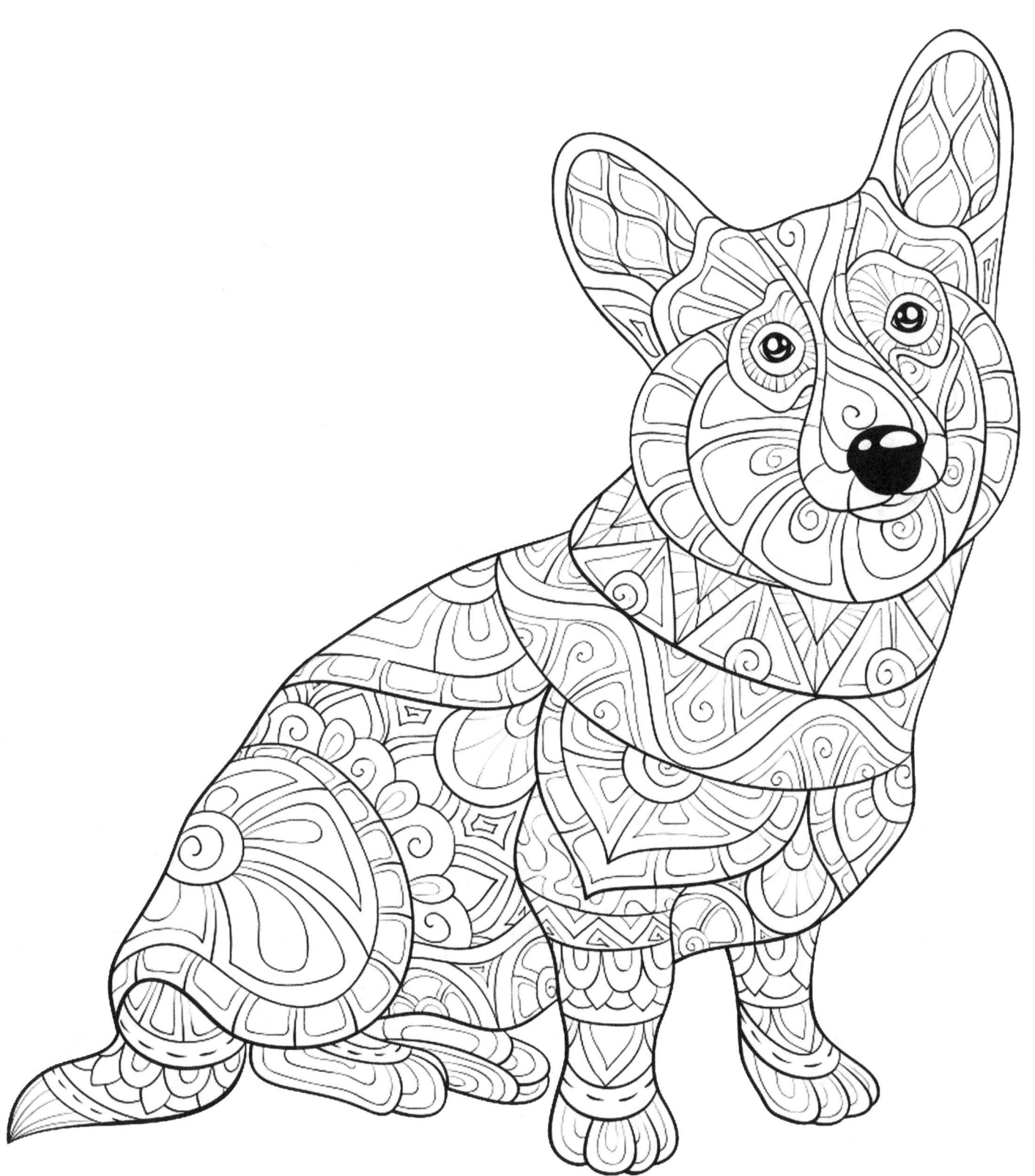

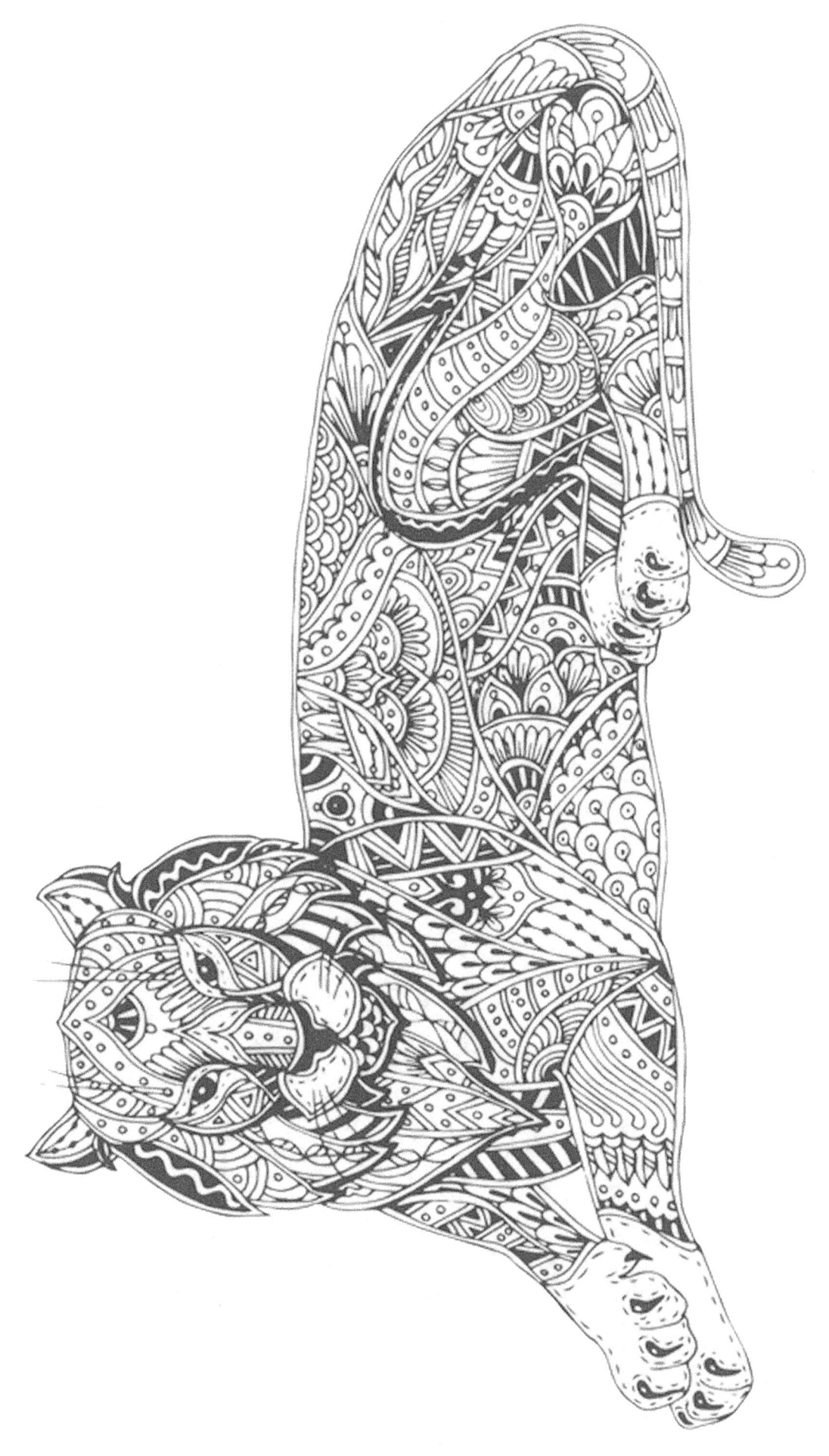

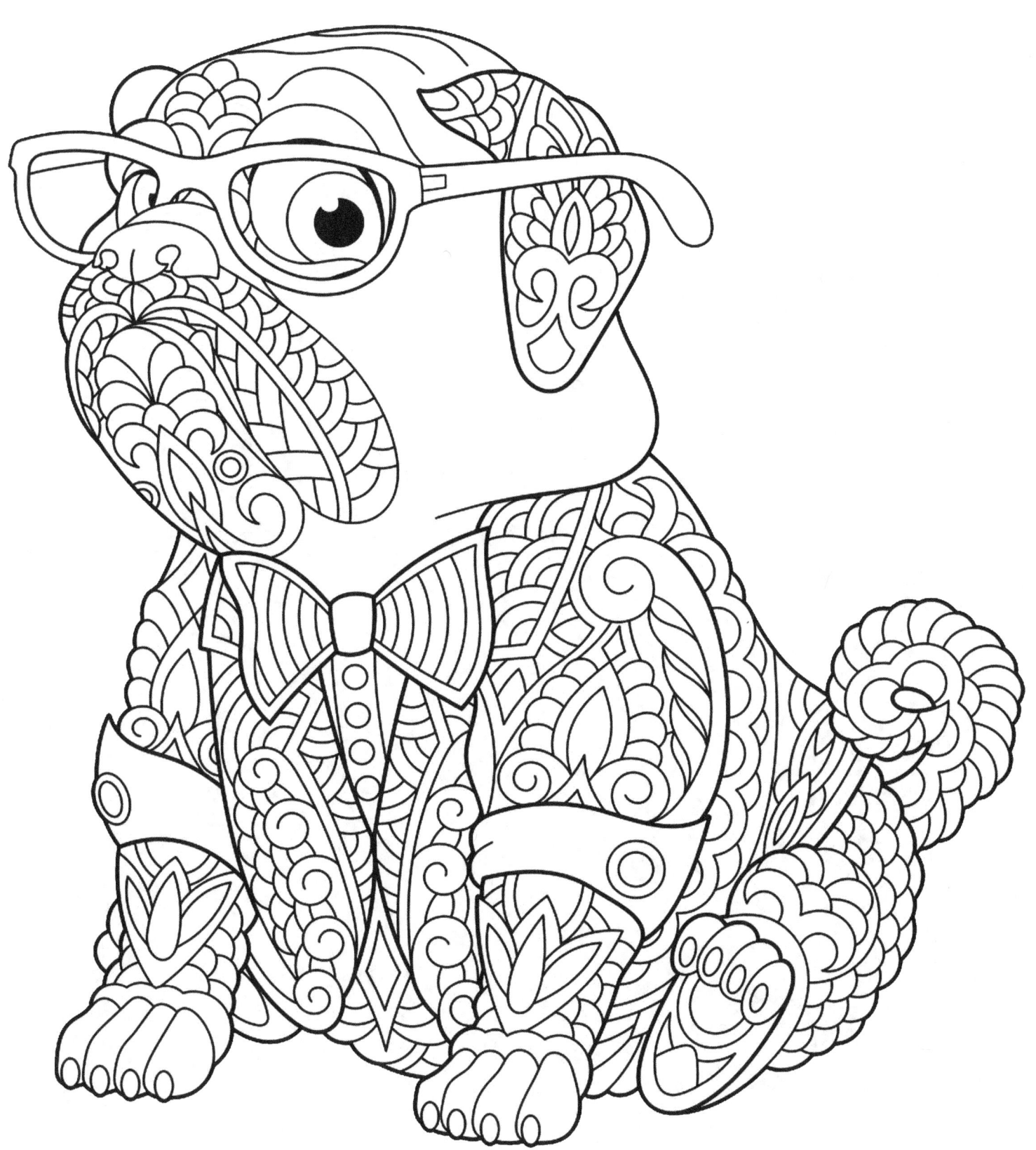

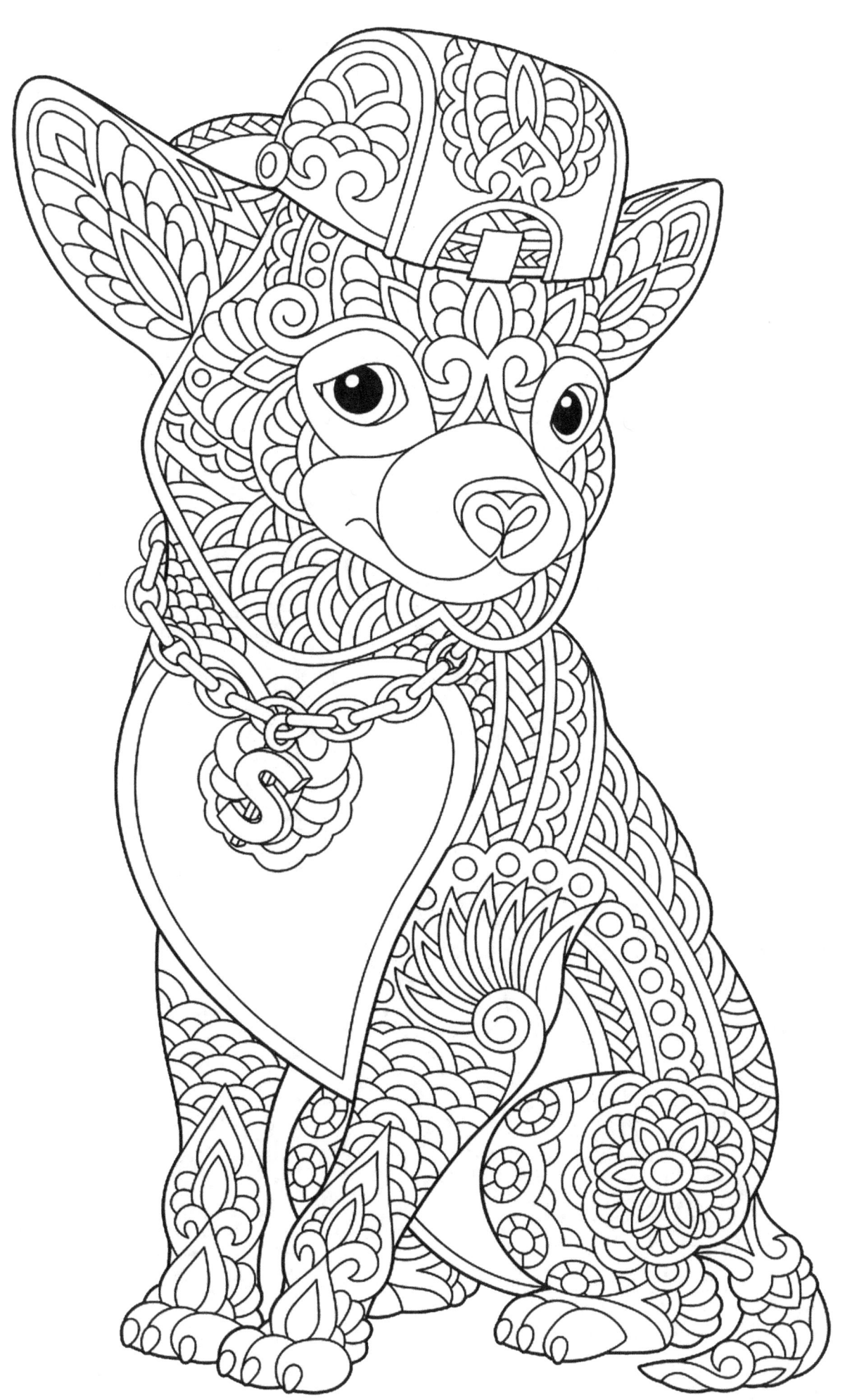

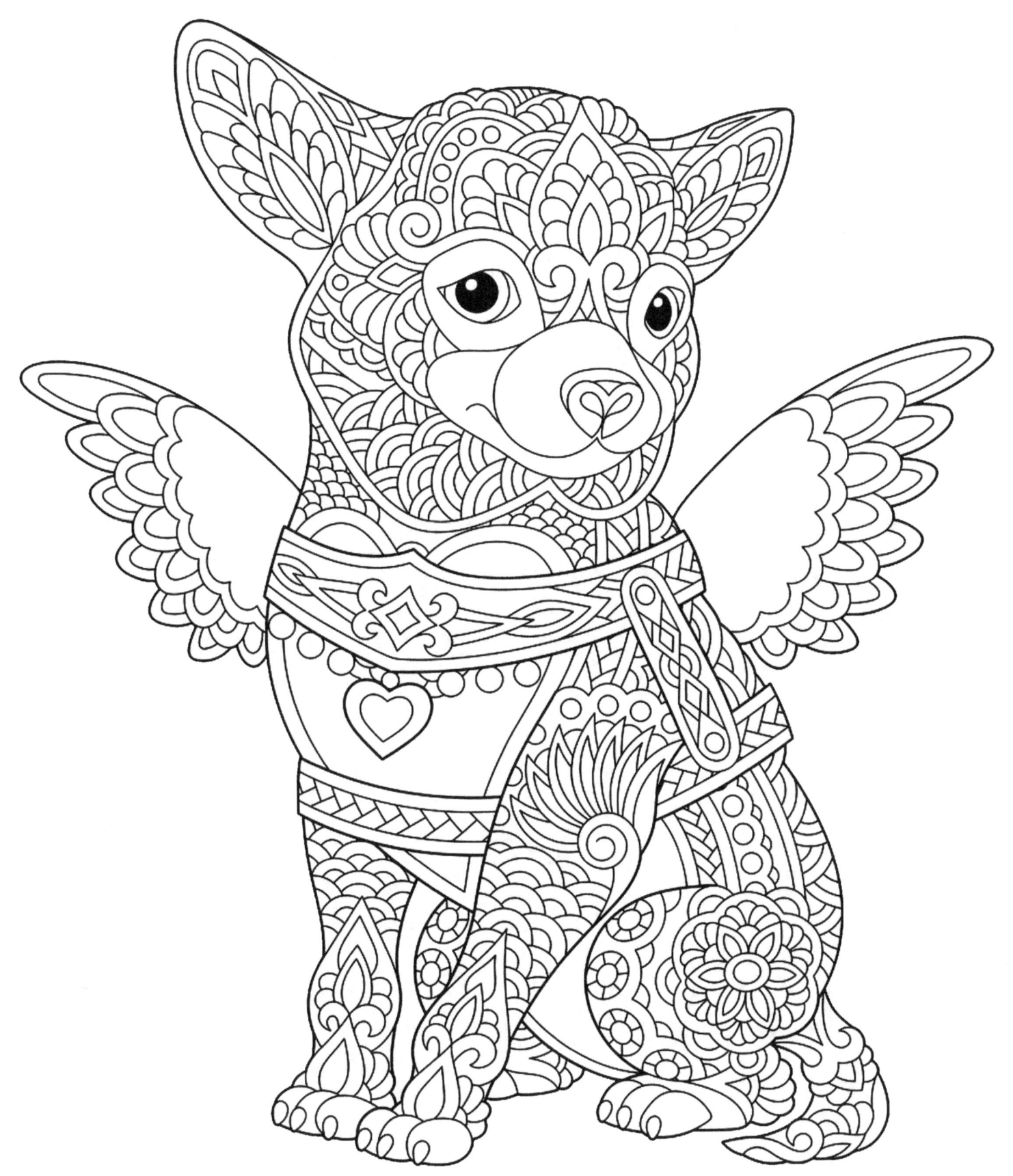

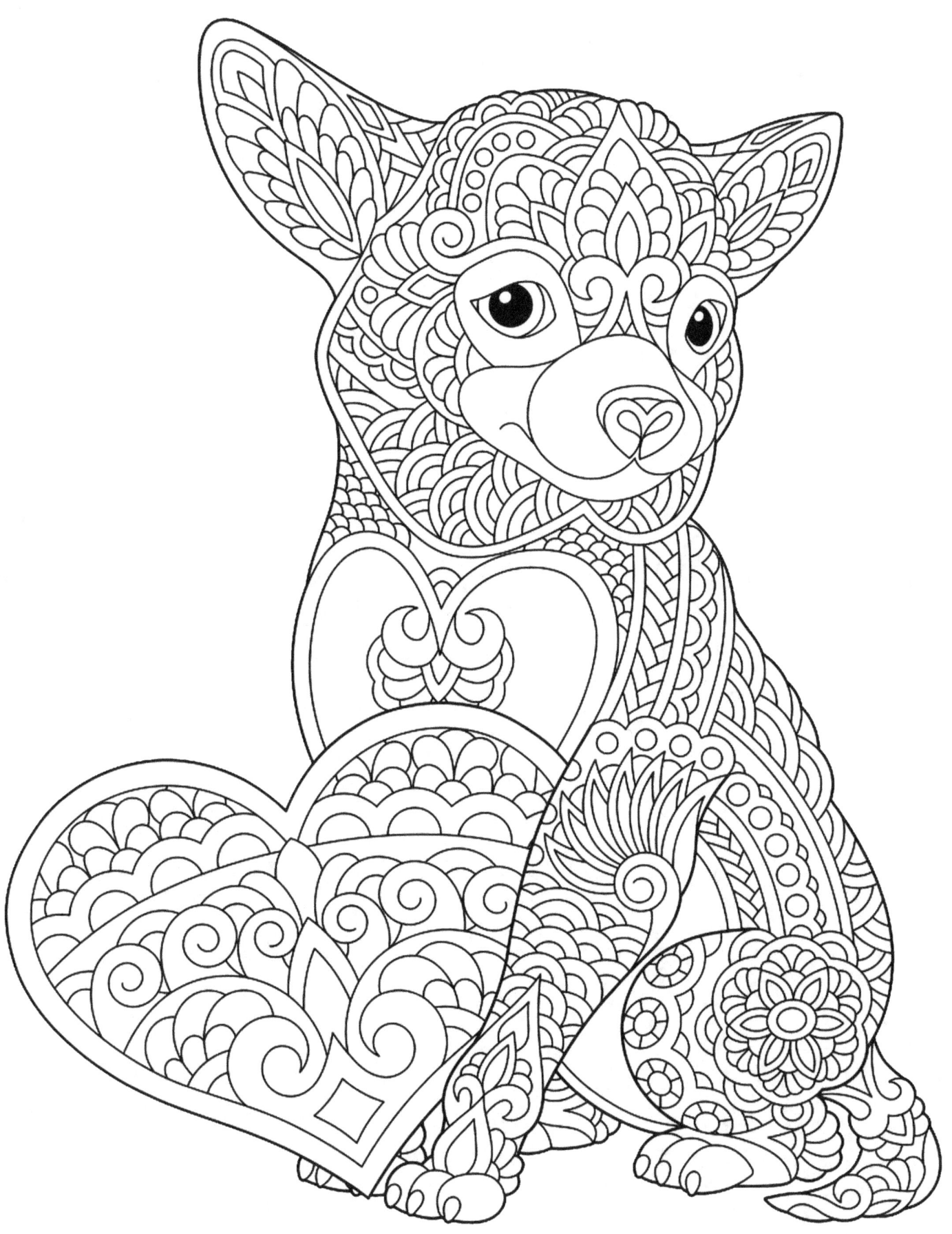

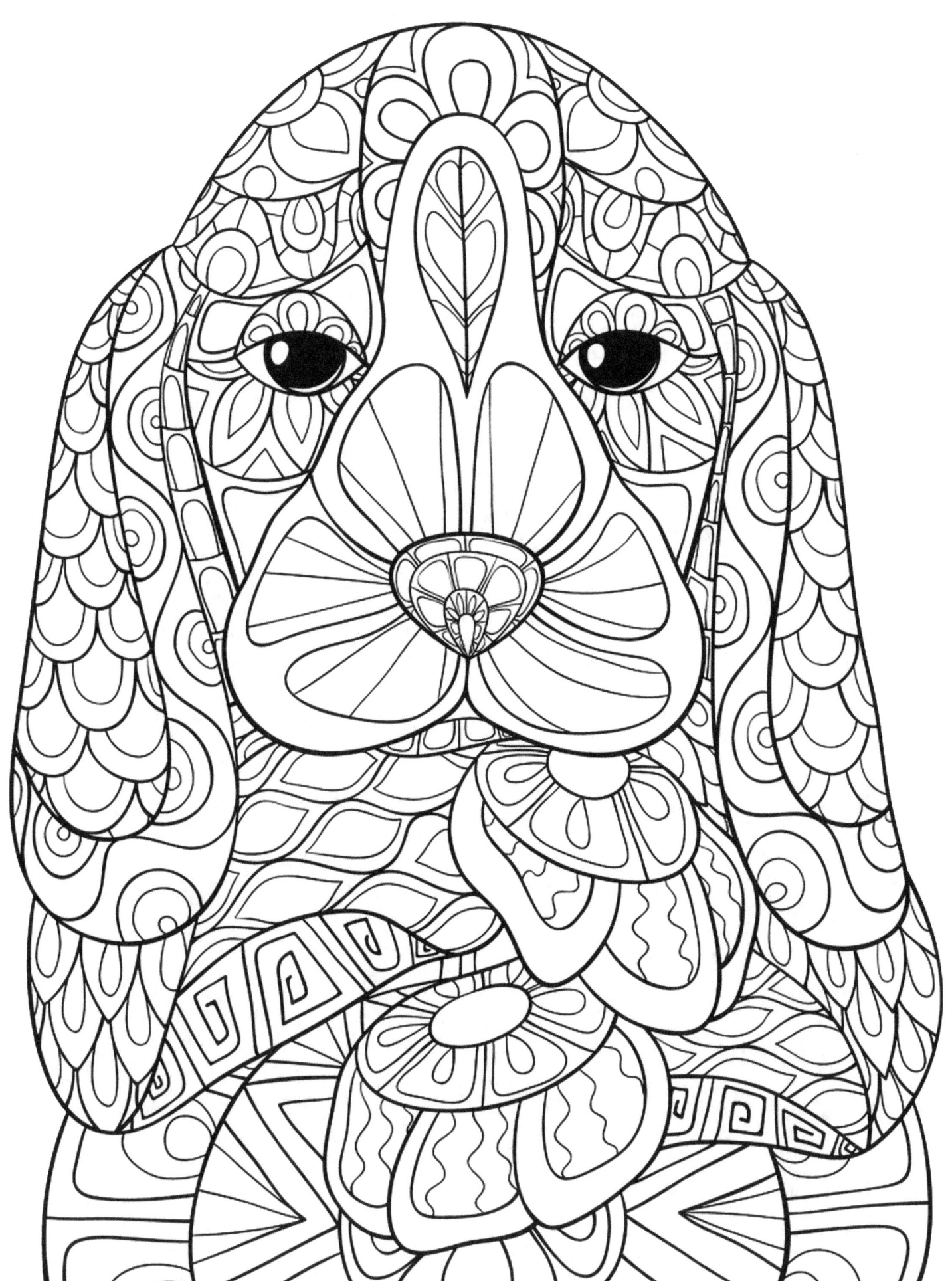

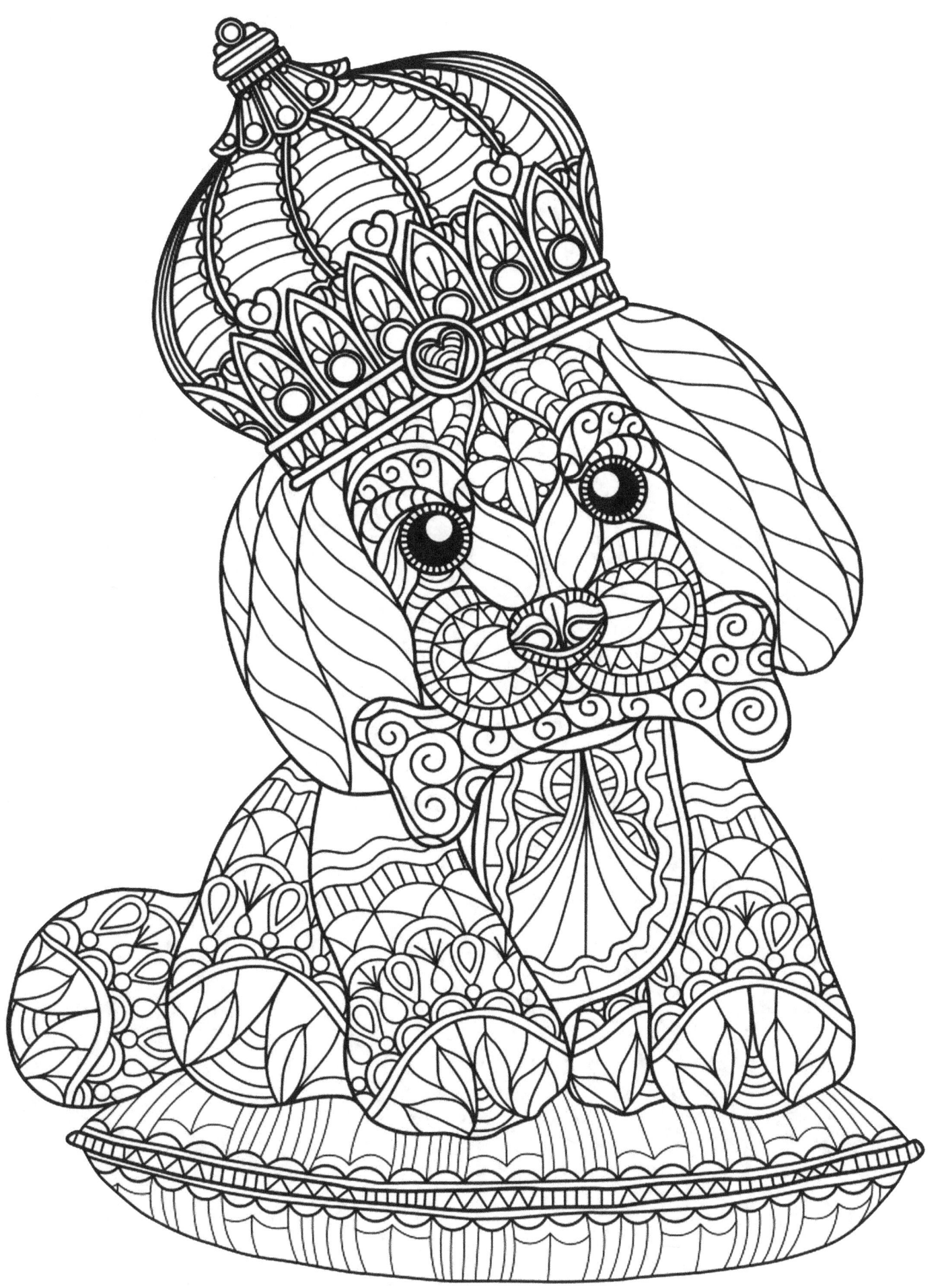

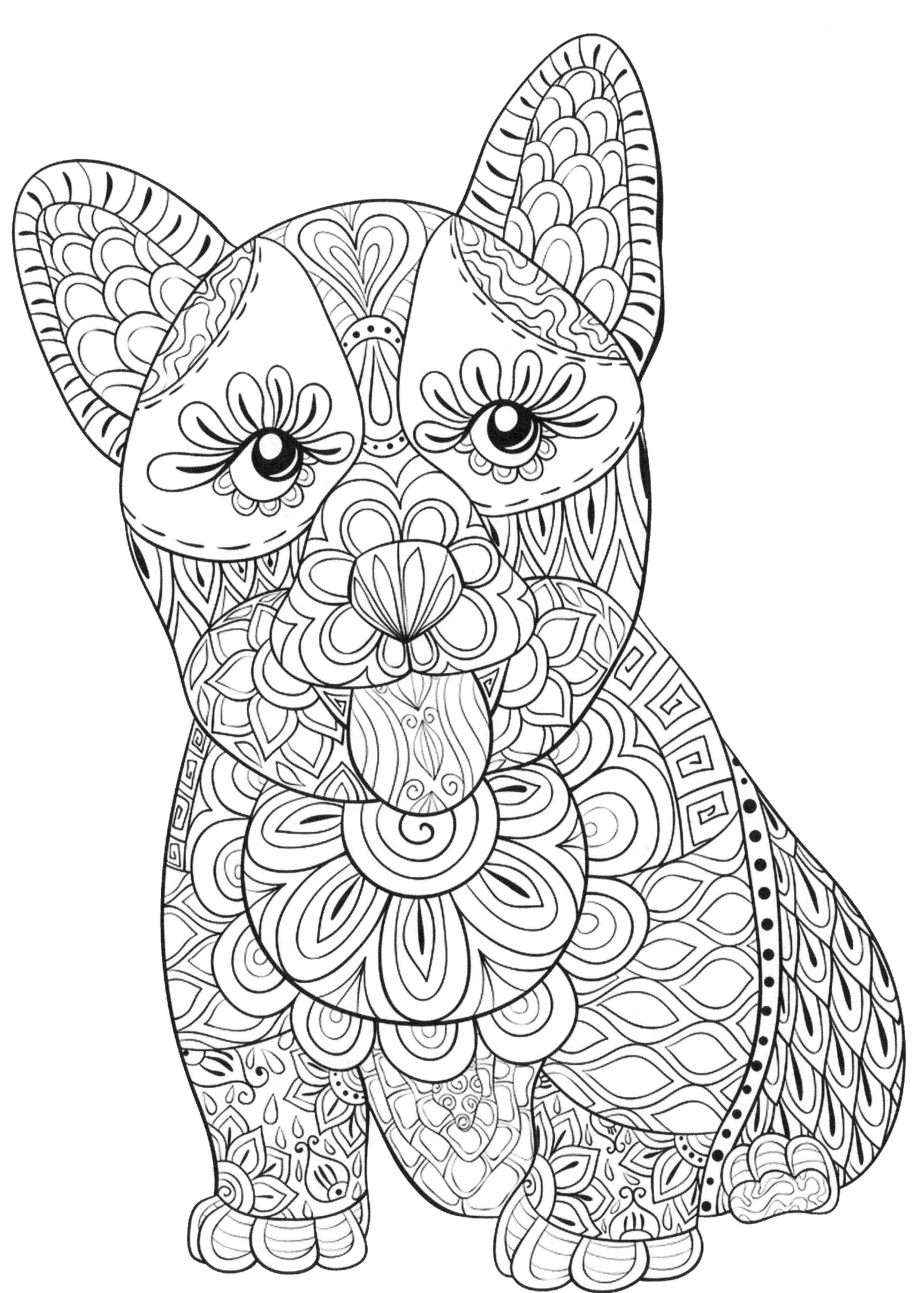

www.ingramcontent.com/pod-product-compliance
Lightning Source LLC
Chambersburg PA
CBHW081101240526
45465CB00026B/3019